First Byte

A practical guide to information technology

Greg Baker
Tom Bowen
adapted and revised by
Rob Austin & Graham Teager

OXFORD UNIVERSITY PRESS 1996

Oxford University Press, Walton Street, Oxford
OX2 6DP
Oxford New York
Athens Auckland Bangkok Bombay
Calcutta Cape Town Dar es Salaam Delhi
Florence Hong Kong Istanbul Karachi
Kuala Lumpur Madras Madrid Melbourne
Mexico City Nairobi Paris Singapore
Taipei Tokyo Toronto
and associated companies in
Berlin and Ibadan

© Oxford University Press, 1996
ISBN 0 19 832286 0
Illustrated by Leigh Hobbs
Typeset and designed by Gecko Ltd,
Bicester, Oxon
Printed in Hong Kong

Contents

Preface

What do you do with a computer?

Imagine you are buying a computer to use at home. What are you going to do with it? Is it for games? Is it to help you with your school work? Are you interested in computer-generated graphics or music? Are you going to write your own games? Do you want to send and receive messages or learn a new language?

A computer is a tool for you to use, like a pen and paper. It will enable you to complete your tasks using many different materials. The computer will make it possible for you to produce high quality work. You can use the computer to make changes to your work and to improve it.

During your time at school, you will see many changes in the types of computers that are used. Computers are getting smaller and are able to carry out a greater range of tasks. They are also taking less time to carry out those tasks.

This book is designed to help you with computer systems that you can use at the moment. At the same time, it provides pointers for the future use of a computer.

The application of computers affect many aspects of daily life. You need to make sure you have the skills to use computers so that they can be of benefit to you.

What skills are needed?

A range of skills are needed to use a computer. You should be able to do the following things:

- start up and shut down a computer
- operate different types of computer software
- use printers and other devices attached to the computer
- use a keyboard to enter words and data
- use a word processor to create reports and stories
- use a spreadsheet to solve problems that use numbers
- access the Internet
- make pictures with paint- and draw-programs
- find information in a database
- make changes to information on a database
- use encyclopaedial and other databases on CD ROM to find information
- create and record your own sounds
- use electronic mail to send and receive messages
- store documents you create for future use

This book will help you learn all these skills.

So, you're using a computer

What tasks can you do with a computer?

Making up your mind about what to do with a computer can be very difficult. Some tasks for which people often use computers are:

- writing a letter
- writing an assignment
- making notes
- creating a budget
- creating a drawing
- creating a family tree
- communicating on the Internet
- composing music
- searching a database to find information
- keeping a list of names, addresses and telephone numbers
- designing a product
- keeping track of friends' birthdays
- playing games
- changing pictures.

Your turn

1 a Where have you used a computer - at school, home, a friend's home, anywhere else? What did you do with the computer? List all the tasks for which you have used a computer.

b List the things that you would like to use a computer for in the future. Use your imagination and try to think of things that computers cannot do at the moment.

What is a computer system?

A computer system is made up of devices which allow you to enter data, process data, store it and then output the results. This is done using a combination of hardware and software.

Completing a task without a computer

If you are writing an assignment for school without a computer you should do the following:

- write a plan listing key points to be included
- use a pen or pencil to assemble ideas on paper to produce a first draft
- revise the assignment making any changes and redraft as necessary
- check the final draft for spelling and other errors
- write out your final copy and hand in.

In doing this you will have carried out the following tasks:

- entered data (that is, the raw material from which we get information) writing with the pen and pencil

- processed that data by arranging and rearranging the words
- stored the data on paper
- presented it for assessment.

You may have redrafted the assignment several times before you are happy with it. Figure 1.1 shows the things you have done.

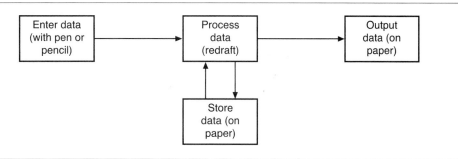

Figure 1.1   Completing a task without a computer

In writing an assignment without a computer, you have used a pen or pencil as an input device, you have processed the data, stored it on paper and then output it on paper. You have used paper to store the work and for output.

Using a computer system

A computer system involves the same process: data is input, processed, stored and then output. Figure 1.2 shows you the steps involved in using a computer to complete a task. A computer system consists of input devices, a computer processor, a storage device and output devices. (Compare Figures 1.1 and 1.2.) The computer system is made up of both hardware and software.

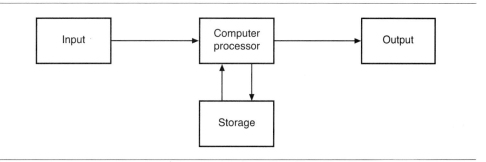

Figure 1.2   How a computer completes a task

Hardware

The hardware consists of the parts you can actually touch, hold and move (with care). This includes the computer processor, a monitor, keyboard and a mouse. Other pieces of hardware that can be attached or built in to a computer are called peripheral devices - these include printers, disk drives, scanners and compact disc drives.

Software

The software is made up of a series of instructions that tell the hardware what to do. The sequence of instructions is called a computer program. You cannot see or touch computer software. It is stored as electronic impulses on floppy disks, hard disks or CD ROM.

Each computer must have an operating system. This software makes the computer usable - it provides a link between the hardware and the person using the computer. When the computer is turned on, the operating system makes sure it starts up correctly.

There are many programs that are used for doing different types of tasks. These include word processors, spreadsheets and drawing programs. This type of software is called applications software.

What makes up the computer?

The computer is made up of a number of parts: a central processing unit, keyboard, monitor, mouse and disk drives.

The computer, keyboard, monitor, mouse and disc drives

Central processing unit (CPU)

The central processing unit (CPU) is the part of the computer where all calculations are carried out and where the instructions are performed. The CPU controls the performance of all other parts of the computer.

The CPU is usually a silicon chip - that is, a small device made of silicon onto which a circuit is printed using a photographic process.

Random access memory (RAM)

Computer memory refers to the internal part of the computer that is used to store instructions and data.

Random access memory (RAM) is that part of the computer in which data and instructions can be stored by the user. When an application is run, instructions are loaded into RAM. Each application requires some of the RAM to work effectively. The amount of memory is measured in kilobytes (Kb), megabytes (Mb) and gigabytes (Gb). One Mb is equal to 1024 Kb and one Gb is equal to 1024 Mb. (One Mb = 300 pages of typed text.) Larger RAM will increase the speed at which the computer will process information.

Read only memory (ROM)

This is the part of a computer on which essential instructions and data for the operating system are recorded. The data may be accessed and used but not altered by the user - that is, it can be looked at but not changed. Large volumes of information are often stored on CD (compact disk) ROM.

When the computer starts up, it first accesses instructions stored in a ROM chip or CD ROM.

Disk storage

The computer includes at least one floppy disk drive for storing data. A floppy disk is made of thin plastic material coated with particles that are magnetised. Data is stored on the disk by using electronic impulses. Floppy disks are inserted and removed from disk drives by the user as needed. A floppy disk usually stores 1.4 Mb of data and is typically 3.5" in diameter.

Most computers also have a hard disk as part of the system. Hard disks are made of metal coated by a magnetic recording material. The disk is fitted into place and cannot be moved. Data is stored on the disk by using electronic impulses. Hard disks can store an almost unlimited quantity of data.

Monitor

A computer monitor is the screen on which the computer displays both input and output. Monochrome monitors use only one colour - often white on black. Some colour monitors can display millions of different colours. Most monitors are colour and display a minimum of 256 colours.

Keyboard

A keyboard is the most common device used for entering data. It looks very much like a typewriter keyboard. When a key is pressed, it is translated into an instruction that the computer can understand.

Mouse

A mouse is a device that is used to control the position of the cursor and to help move around a computer screen. It can be used to carry out many commands by pointing and clicking the mouse buttons.

What can be attached to a computer?

A peripheral device is anything that is external to the computer that can be attached to the computer or built into the case which contains the CPU. Devices which are often attached to computers include:

- printers
- extra disk drives
- scanners
- microphones
- compact disk drives
- modems.

Input/output devices

The devices listed above can all be used as either input or output devices. An input device is used to transfer data into a computer. For example, a scanner can be used to enter data in the form of a diagram. A microphone can be used to enter sounds.

An output device is used to present data that is transferred *from* a computer. A printer is used to display an assignment that has been written using a computer. Speakers can play sounds that have been recorded on a computer.

Your turn

1 Find out information about computers to which you have access at:
   a school
   b home or at a neighbour's or relative's home
   c the workplace of one of your parent's or another adult you know.

Try to answer the following questions:

- What is the size of the monitor? Is it colour or monochrome?
- How many keys are there on the keyboard?
- What input devices does it use?
- What output devices does it use?
- How much RAM (random access memory) does it have?
- What is the capacity, in Mb, of the hard disk?
- How many floppy disk drives does it have?

Personal computers

There are two types of computers used in schools - desktop, and laptop or notebook.

Desktop computers

These computers are designed to be used in the one place on the top of a desk. When personal computers were first developed desktop computers were the only type that were made.

Notebook computers

A notebook computer is small and light enough to be carried around in a bag. It includes a battery so that it can operate without having to be connected to a power point.

The most important advantage of these computers is that they can be used almost anywhere - at school, at home, in a local library, on a bus, in a train or a car or sitting on a park bench. Many people who travel a lot in their jobs use notebook computers so that they can continue to work when away from their office and transfer their work or output by linking to the appropriate devices upon return.

What about software?

A computer will not work without software. Software provides the instructions to the computer that allow you to do any of the tasks listed earlier.

Most computer systems include the operating system software when they are bought. Other software packages must be bought separately.

Types of software

Different types of computer programs have been written to carry out specific tasks. For example, computer programs have been written for each of the following categories:

- communications
- computer-aided design (CAD)
- database
- management
- games
- page layout (desktop publishing)
- simulations
- music composing
- spreadsheets
- word processing
- programming
- graphics
- integrated packages commonly including word processor, database, spreadsheet and communications).

Your turn

1 List both the categories of software and the names of packages that are used at your school. For example, your school will probably have IBM-compatible computers and use MS Office as an integrated package, with Word 6 as a word processor and Excel 6 as a spread sheet. All these applications will run under Windows 95.
2 Look at a newspaper advertisement for computer software and write down the name and price of a piece of software for each of the above categories.
3 Add another five categories of computer software to the above list.
4 Find the names of six companies that produce software for the personal computer market.

Review questions

1 There are four main tasks involved in computing. What are they? You should include a diagram as part of your answer.
2 What is the difference between software and hardware?
3 Why is software so important?
4 The following abbreviations refer to parts of a computer system: CPU, RAM, ROM, CD. Explain what the abbreviations stand for and the main function of each of these parts.
5 What is a peripheral device? Give examples of three peripheral devices that are used at your school.
6 What is an input device? List four different input devices.
7 What is an output device? List four different output devices.

Tasks

1 See if you can find someone who uses a notebook computer and find out what he or she thinks are the advantages and disadvantages of using it compared to using a desktop computer.
2 Imagine you are going to buy a computer. What are the three most important tasks for which you would use the computer? What software packages would be needed to do those tasks? What computer hardware would you like to buy? Would you buy an IBM-compatible, an Apple Macintosh or some other computer type? Give three reasons for your choice. (If you already own a computer, answer these questions from your own experience.)
3 Investigate the types of computers in your school library and your local library. List the peripheral devices that are used in each library. Find out what the most frequently used applications are.

Operating a computer

How do you start up a computer?

To start up a computer you will need to:

- Turn on the power to the computer and the monitor and any peripherals. You will need to find where the switches are on the computer.
- If the computer has an inbuilt hard disk, you need do nothing else but wait for the computer to start up.
- If the computer is connected to a network you will need to log on (gain entry) to the network.

What happens when you start up a computer?

When a computer is turned on it carries out some instructions that are located in its ROM (read only memory). It then checks the disk drives for disks in the following order: first floppy disks, then hard disks.

As soon as it locates operating system files, it starts up.

Start up actions

During start up a number of instructions are carried out. These vary according to the type of computer. The typical sequence of events when starting up a computer is shown in Figure 2.1 (page 10).

How do you restart a computer?

Every computer will need to be restarted from time to time when errors occur. Typical errors are:

- a system crash with an error message
- no response from the keyboard
- a frozen screen where nothing appears to happen.

For an IBM-compatible PC, the following methods should be tried in order:

- press the CONTROL, ALT and DELETE keys together
- press the RESET button
- turn the power off, leave for 30 seconds and turn the power on again. (This should only be done as a last resort.)

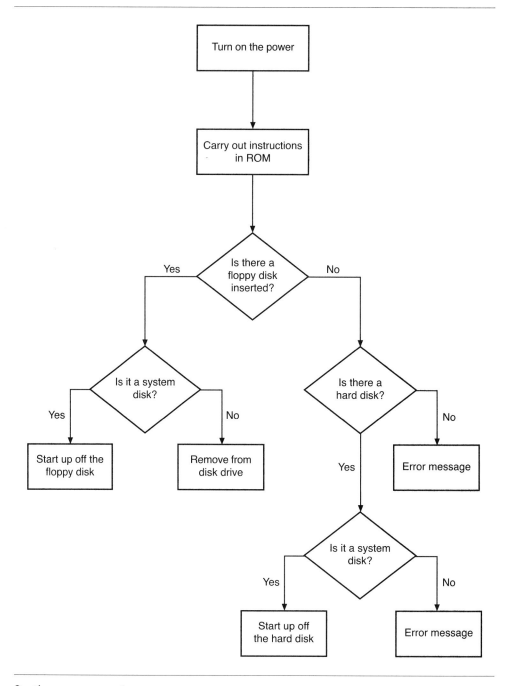

Figure 2.1   Starting up a computer

For an Apple Macintosh, do one of the following:
- press the key combination that restarts the computer (check the manual)
- press the RESET key at the back left-hand side of the computer (on some models)
- turn the power off, leave for 30 seconds and turn the power on again. (This should only be done as a last resort.)

A computer should never be turned off or restarted when it is accessing a disk, as it is likely to damage the disk. A light usually flashes to show that a disk is being accessed.

If a computer 'hangs' – that is, it stops processing – you may need to restart it. In this case, you are likely to lose any changes you have made since you last saved your work. To restart the computer, you can use a special combination of keys, for example, CONTROL/ALT/DELETE on IBM compatibles, or press the RESET button.

What happens if the computer does not start?

If the computer does not start, check the following:

- Are the power cords to the computer and monitor connected properly? Is the power turned on?
- Are the cables between the parts of the computer system properly connected?
- Are the lights on the monitor turned on? Are the lights on the disk drive turned on?

If the computer still does not start you should:

- Start up using another floppy disk that has a system installed. You should always have a floppy disk on hand that can be used to start up the computer.
- Seek the assistance of a computer teacher or support person.

Figure 2.2 (on page 12) shows the steps that should be carried out.

Your turn

1 Start up a computer and write down the things that happen. Watch the screen carefully for messages.
2 Locate the keys that will restart the computer without turning off the power. Restart the computer using those keys.
3 Where is the switch to turn on the power to: the computer; the monitor?

What is a file?

A file is a collection of related data. Every time you create and save a document, you create a file.

With a computer, each document that is created is stored electronically on a computer disk. The file can be recognised by its name. There are many different types of computer files. Each application creates its own type of file. In Figure 2.3 (on page 12), each file has a name - for example, all the files with 'doc' after their name (the file extension) are word processing documents.

When a file is first saved to a disk, it is given a name. That name must follow the rules of the operating system. Files may be renamed by using the appropriate command in the operating system.

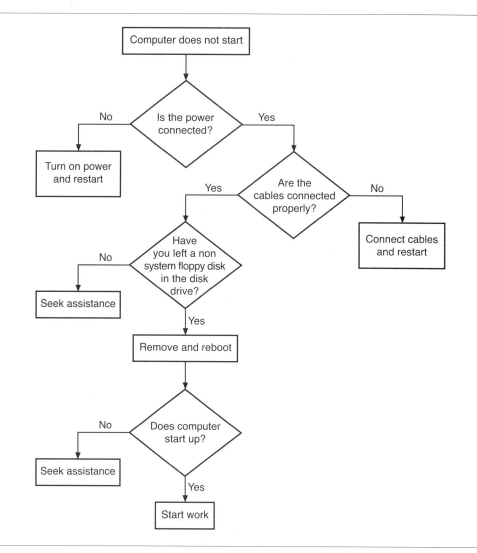

Figure 2.2   What if the computer does not start up?

Figure 2.3   An example of a computer screen listing of files

Interacting with the computer

The way in which people make commands that are used by the computer to carry out useful tasks is called the 'user interface'.

These are commands used by MS-DOS, which is an example of a command line operating system.

◆ Icon-based – commands are carried out using a keyboard and mouse with pull down menus and by clicking on icons. An icon is a small symbol that represents a file or directory. The Macintosh operating system and Microsoft Windows are examples of icon-based operating systems. Figure 2.4 shows icons representing directories in Microsoft Windows.

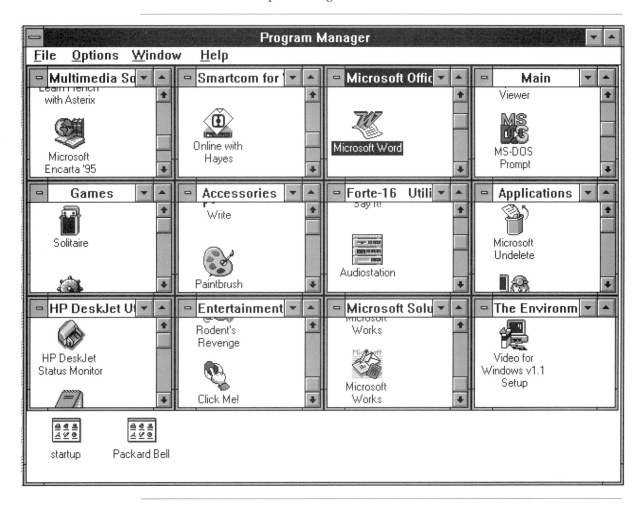

Figure 2.4 Icons which represent files in a Windows environment

Managing your files

A directory is a table of contents of files on a disk or part of a disk. Directories are used to organise and store files.

Files often need to be copied, deleted, renamed or moved. This type of operation is carried out in a package which lets you see the files in any directory, their size, content and when they were last worked on. 'File Manager' is a Windows application that lets you work with files in this way.

On PC's directory icons look like folders that are used in a filing cabinet. See the clipart directory in Figure 2.3.

A listing of the files in a directory gives the file name, type, size and date of creation or modification. Files can be listed in different ways - by name, size, date or type. Refer to a manual to find out how to list the files in these different ways.

Your turn

1 How do you find a directory of files on the computer you use?
2 Look at a directory of files on a disk on a computer. How many files are in the directory? What are the different types of files?
3 Look at a directory of files in order of size, from largest to smallest. What other ways are there to look at files and their content?

Computer housekeeping tasks

A number of tasks need to be carried out to ensure effective operation of a computer. These include:

◆ formatting disks
◆ creating, naming and renaming files
◆ copying files and disks
◆ deleting files
◆ creating directories
◆ finding files on a disk or in a directory
◆ printing files
◆ looking at the contents of a file.

The manual that comes with the computer provides a detailed description of the functions of an operating system.

The operating system

The operating system is the software that enables you to carry out housekeeping tasks. Every computer must have an operating system.

The operating system is the first program that is run when the computer is started up.

Formatting a floppy disk

Each disk must be formatted before it can be used. The format of a disk is the way in which the data is to be arranged on that disk. Each type of operating system has a different format.

When a new floppy disk is purchased, it may not be recognised by a computer. The process of formatting allows the computer to recognise the disk.

Organising files

Disks are usually organised into directories to make it easier to manage files. Directories are created to store related files and to make them easier to find. This is similar to organising documents into cardboard files and storing them in a filing cabinet.

Your turn

1 Find out how to do the following tasks. Carry out each of the tasks and write down what you had to do.
   a Format a floppy disk.
   b Create a directory.
   c Copy a file from one disk to another disk.
   d Delete a file from a disk.
   e Copy the contents of one disk to another disk.
   f Find the most recently created file.
   g Show the contents of a file on the monitor.
   h Print out the contents of a file on a printer.

How is data stored?

Your data will be saved on a disk. If you have a hard disk, your files can be stored on this. If you are working on a network, your work may be stored on a network hard disk.

What is a floppy disk?

A floppy disk is a medium for storing data. It consists of a circular piece of thin plastic material that is coated with particles which can be magnetised. The circular plastic is the disk, which is stored in a protective jacket. The most commonly used disk size is 3.5" in diameter.

The disk is divided into a number of tracks and the data is recorded on the tracks by electronic impulses. When a disk is inserted in a disk drive, the disk is rotated by the drive. Read/write heads are positioned over the tracks to sense or create electronic impulses on the disk which represent data.

Floppy disks include a write protect notch or lever which prevents data being erased or overwritten accidentally.

The usual capacity of a High Density floppy disk is 1.4 Mb.

What is a hard disk?

A hard disk is made up of one or more rigid metal platters that are coated with material that allows data to be magnetically recorded. The disks rotate at very high speeds, for example at 3600 revolutions per second, and have read/write heads that move across the disk surface.

Hard disks can store more data than floppy disks. The smallest size now usually installed is 500 Mb. They access the data more quickly than floppy disks can.

Backing up – protecting your work

A backup of a file is a copy of that file stored on another disk. A backup is needed in case something goes wrong with the original disk on which a file is store.

Backup disks need to be carefully labelled and dated and safely stored to ensure they are readily available when needed. At least two copies of every important file should be kept.

Copies of original software should always be made before installing or starting to use that software. The original disks should be stored in a safe place and not used for everyday work.

In general you should back up early and back up often!

Get into the habit of backing up work every ten minutes or so to ensure a minimum of work is lost. Always back up a file before printing it in case something goes wrong in the printing process.

Looking after floppy disks

It is easy to damage a disk and thus lose the data stored on it. The following is a list of guidelines for preventing damage:

- ◆ Do not put magnetised items near disks, for example, telephone handsets.
- ◆ Do not put disk on the top of disk drives.
- ◆ Do not fold or bend the disks.
- ◆ Do not touch the surface of the disk or the shutter on 3.5" disks.
- ◆ Keep the disk away from extreme heat or sunlight (for example, car seat on a hot day).
- ◆ Do not keep the disk in a container with dust.
- ◆ Do not put heavy objects on disks.

When travelling, disks should not be put through X-ray machines at airports as these may damage the data.

Disk labels are usually provided with the disks when purchased. The label is stuck onto the disk and the contents of the disk can then be written on the label. Be careful not to write on the disk cover with a sharp pen or pencil.

Disk manufacturers give a guarantee of quality and will replace faulty disks.

Your turn

1 Do the computers you use at school have hard disks? If so, what is the storage capacity of them?
2 Find out what your school does about backing up the files on the computers which you use. Answer the following questions:

- ◆ How often are the files backed up?
- ◆ What medium is used for backup purposes - floppy disks, hard disks, magnetic tape?
- ◆ Who carries out the backups?
- ◆ How often are backups needed?

What about printers?

Printers are used to print both text and graphics that have been generated by a computer. The type of printer to be used depends on the following:

- the quality of the printing needed
- the speed of printing needed
- colour or black and white
- noise requirements
- cost of the printer – to buy and to run
- the type of paper to be printed on
- the type and quality of graphics to be printed.

Printers need software to communicate with a computer. The software is usually installed as part of the operating system of the computer for example, the Windows version is called Print Manager.

Your turn

1 What type of printers are you able to use at school? Classify them as being dot matrix, ink jet, laser or any other type. How quickly can these printers print?
2 Many printers have different quality options - for example, draft or proof. Print out a file with the different settings available on a printer. Check the different quality of the print and how long they take to print.

What is a computer virus?

A virus is a computer program that attaches itself to other computer programs. Once it is attached, it causes damage to files. A virus is spread when a disk containing a virus is inserted into the disk drive of a computer. The virus copies itself onto the hard disk of the computer.

Why worry about a virus?

A computer virus can damage files on a disk. It can be selective or it can affect every file. A virus can cause random system crashes and work can be lost.

What can be done to combat the spread of viruses?

The use of anti virus software can combat the spread of viruses.
This can work by:

- scanning – each time a disk is inserted, it is scanned to see if it has a known virus

- checking – run a virus checking program regularly to check the files on a disk and take action if any are found.

Other precautions include:

- not borrowing disks from other people – whenever you borrow a disk you run the risk of infecting your computer

- being wary of public domain and and shareware programs
- purchasing and using only commercial software.

Virus protection software needs to be updated regularly. As new viruses are detected, the software is altered to check for these viruses.

Your turn

Have any viruses been detected on computers at your school? What problems do they create? What precautions are taken to prevent the spread of viruses?

Who owns software?

Software for computers is created by specialist programmers and is original work, just like a book or film. Commercial software is produced by programmers for software publishers. It is illegal for copies of software to be made without authorisation. An authorised copy can be made if the software publisher allows a backup copy of the original disks.

Do you own the software when you pay for it?

Purchase of the software does not give you the right of ownership of the code that makes up the software. The software is, in effect, leased to you and can be used according to the conditions of the contract. Often the software is provided in a sealed packet with the licence printed on the outside. By breaking the seal you are agreeing to the conditions of the contract.

Copy protection of software

Computer software publishers try to prevent unauthorised copying and use of their programs. Unauthorised copying of software is called software 'piracy'. There are severe penalties under copyright law for those who make and those who sell 'pirated' copies of software. Some software is 'copy protected' to make it harder to pass on copies. Some firms have a policy of using copy protection, others only use 'copyright law'. Publishers would prefer not to use copy protection but see no other way to protect their interests.

Your turn

1 Do you think 'copy protection' is a good idea? Give reasons for your answer.

2 If you purchased a piece of computer software, would you copy protect your work? Give reasons for your answer.

Review questions

1 What is a file?

2 List the objects that make up a computer network.

3 What is an operating system?

4 Compare two different types of user interface. Which do you prefer and why?

5 If a computer will not start, what should you check to find out what is wrong?

6 How do you print a list of files in a directory on the screen of the computer you use?

7 How do you create a new directory on the computer you use at school?

8 Why are backups of files important?

Tasks

1 Find out what different operating systems can work with the computers you use at school.

2 Find out the prices of floppy disks from a newspaper. How much does a 3.5″ disk cost? Compare the prices of three different brands. Compare the prices of high density and double sided disks. Is there a difference in price between brand name disks and those with no brand name?

3 Obtain a copy of a warranty for a floppy disk. Under what conditions will the company that makes the disk replace it? For how long is the warranty in force?

4 Compare the prices of the following types of printer that can be connected to the computer you use: dot matrix printer; ink jet printer; laser printer.

5 Find out which pieces of software at your school have copy protection. How are they protected? Does it make it more difficult to use the software?

6 From a copy of a software licence find out:
   a What does the licence allow you to do?
   b Under what conditions can you copy the software?
   c What are the obligations of the software company?

Using a keyboard

How important is the keyboard to the operation of a computer?

A keyboard is used to:

◆ communicate with a computer (telling it what to do)

◆ enter information into a computer (for example, to write a story).

A computer responds to instructions. By pressing a single key or a combination of keys a message is sent to the computer.

What are the keys on a keyboard?

Keyboards usually have approximately 102 to 105 keys. Many keyboards have a keypad with numbers on the right-hand side. This is called a numeric keypad.

Keys can be separated into the following categories:

◆ letter keys – **a** to **z**, **A** to **Z**
◆ number keys – **0** to **9**
◆ punctuation keys – for example, full stop, comma, colon – **. , :**
◆ cursor keys – up, down, left, right – ↑ ↓ → ←

◆ symbol keys – for example, **%**, **&**
◆ special keys – for example, ENTER, ESCAPE, ALT, COMMAND, PAGE UP, PAGE DOWN
◆ function keys – F1 to F15, which carry out specific tasks.

What is a 'QWERTY' keyboard?

The standard keyboard for computers is known as a 'QWERTY' keyboard. The term 'QWERTY' refers to the location of the first six letters on the top letter row. The position of the number keys (1 to 0) and the letter keys (A to Z) is the same for most keyboards. Figure 3.1 shows the characters of the basic keyboard.

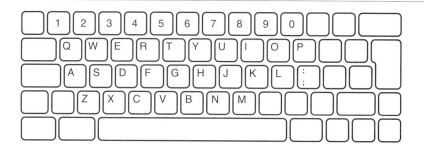

Figure 3.1 QWERTY keyboard layout.

Your turn

1 Where are the keys 'QWERTY' located on the keyboard?
2 What keys surround the QWERTY keys on your keyboard?
3 How many keys are on your keyboard?
4 What are the 'special keys' on the keyboard which are not identified in Figure 3.1? See if you can find the following keys:

- ◆ ENTER
- ◆ SPACEBAR
- ◆ SHIFT (left and right)
- ◆ CAPS LOCK
- ◆ CURSOR or ARROW (up, down, right, left)
- ◆ DELETE and/or BACKSPACE
- ◆ TAB.

Upper and lower case letters

Letter keys can produce either a capital letter (upper case) or a small letter (lower case). For example, the 'A' key can produce either 'a' or 'A'. Keys are shown on a keyboard as capital letters, as in Figure 3.1, but when pressed will produce a lower case letter. For example, the following line is typed in lower case:

this is typed in lower case.

How is an upper case letter produced?

To type an upper case letter you use the 'CAPS LOCK' key or the 'SHIFT' key, as shown in Figure 3.2.

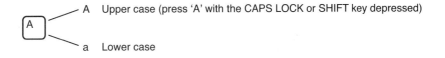

Figure 3.2   Upper and lower case letter 'A'

The following line is typed in upper case:

THIS IS TYPED IN UPPER CASE.

Capital letters can only be produced by holding down the SHIFT key or with the CAPS LOCK key down as you press the key.

Using the CAPS LOCK key

The CAPS LOCK key 'locks' the letter keys as capitals. With this setting, all letter keys (A – Z) are typed as upper case. The CAPS LOCK key only affects the letter keys, all other keys remain as normal.

Your turn

1 Locate the CAPS LOCK key. Is the key up or down? What happens when you press the key? Does your keyboard have a light to show when the key is down? Put the key in its up position.
2 Find the 'A' key and press it. Does 'a' or 'A' appear on screen? If the letter 'A' appears on screen then the CAPS LOCK is down, not up.
3 Find the number '1' key and press it. What is the character that appears on screen?

Why use lower case letters?

When reading we recognise letters by their shape. The shapes made by the letters are more distinctive in lower case. Words and sentences in capital letters should be used only for special effect, such as a short heading. The following lines illustrate the difference:

Words and sentences typed in lower case letters are easy to read.

WORDS AND SENTENCES TYPED IN CAPITAL LETTERS ARE DIFFICULT TO READ.

Our eyes recognise letters by following their shape, so sentences with lower case characters, which have ascenders (e.g. 'd') and descenders (e.g. 'y'), are easier to read.

Your turn

1 Type your name and address in upper case, then in lower case. Which is easier to read?
2 Which letters in particular make it easy to read lower case letters?

Using the SHIFT key

To type a single upper case character requires a SHIFT key to be pressed at the same time as the letter key is pressed. Figure 3.3 shows the characters that would be created with the SHIFT key depressed.

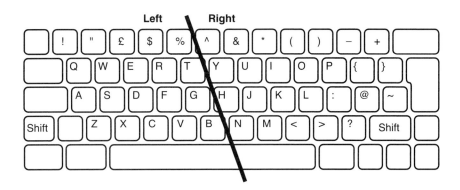

Left SHIFT key is depressed for upper case characters on right side of keyboard

Right SHIFT key is depressed for upper case characters on left side of keyboard

Figure 3.3   QWERTY keyboard (upper case characters using the SHIFT keys)

 Your turn

The following keys may also be on your keyboard. See if you can find the following keys: CONTROL, ALT, ESCAPE, PAGE UP, PAGE DOWN, HOME, END, Function keys (F1 to F12 or F15 depending on the keyboard), NUMLOCK, SCROLL, PAUSE, BREAK, PRINT SCREEN, INSERT.

Numbers, punctuation marks, symbols and other characters

Some keys have two characters printed on the key face – for example, Figure 3.4 shows the number 3 on the top row which has the £ symbol above it. The number 3 is the lower case and the £ symbol is the upper case.

£ Upper case

3 Upper case

Figure 3.4   Number 3 and £ key

On a computer keyboard there is a difference between the capital 'O' and zero '0'. Similarly with lower case letter 'l' and number '1'.

Table 3.1 (on page 24) shows the punctuation marks and symbols located on most keyboards. Included in the table is the rule about the general formatting of the mark or symbol.

When using a computer, only one space is required after most punctuation marks.

Table 3.1   Punctuation and symbol marks

Punctuation marks	Name	General formatting	
•	full stop (sometimes called a period)	space once after	
,	comma	space once after	
:	colon	space once after	
;	semi-colon	space once after	
?	question mark	space once after	
' ' open closed	single quotation mark	no space between marks and words inside quotation marks	
" " open closed	double quotation mark (use when necessary to show a quote within a quote)	no space between marks and words inside quotation marks	
!	exclamation mark	space once after	
'	apostrophe	no spacing	
( ) left right	parenthesis (also called brackets)	no space between marks and words inside brackets	
/	forward slash	no space before or after	
—	dash	no space before or after	
-	hyphen	no spacing either side	
Mathematical signs/symbols	Below are some simple examples of mathematical signs. Some word processors can set out complex mathematical equations.		
=	equals	$8 \times 3 = 24$	one space either side
+	plus	$8 + 3 = 11$	one space either side

Your turn

1 Locate the following keys. Do you need to press SHIFT to produce the character?

. full stop – also sometimes called a period

? question mark

, comma

£ pound sign

2 Find out where the various marks and symbols from Table 3.1 are located on your computer keyboard.

Special and unusual symbols

Figure 3.5 Some of the symbols available with some fonts

Keyboards can be set up to produce characters such as those shown in Figure 3.5 when the appropriate font is installed. Pressing SHIFT produces another set of characters. Figure 3.6 shows the graphic characters that can be created with the Wingdings font.

Lower case: **Upper case:**

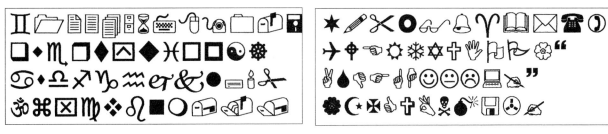

Figure 3.6 Keyboard characters with Wingdings font

Special keys

There are also keys for special tasks. Figure 3.7 (on page 26) shows the various special keys. The names will be different depending on the computer. These special keys may be called OPTION, COMMAND, RESET, CONTROL, ESCAPE and ALT. For example, the BACKSPACE key might appear on another computer keyboard as the DELETE key. BACKSPACE moves the cursor one space to the left; DELETE will remove the character to the right of the cursor.

Often these special keys will have a special shape to make them easier to see and touch – for example, CAPS LOCK and ENTER are larger than the letter and number keys.

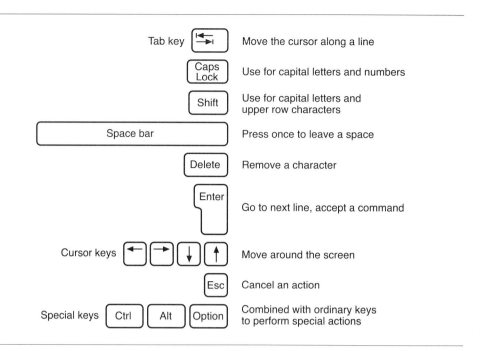

Tab key — Move the cursor along a line

Caps Lock — Use for capital letters and numbers

Shift — Use for capital letters and upper row characters

Space bar — Press once to leave a space

Delete — Remove a character

Enter — Go to next line, accept a command

Cursor keys — Move around the screen

Esc — Cancel an action

Special keys — Ctrl, Alt, Option — Combined with ordinary keys to perform special actions

Figure 3.7 **Special keys and their purpose**

The use of a special key can vary according to the software – for example, TAB for a word processor could set text to a position on a line, on a database it could move the cursor to the next field and for a spreadsheet it could move the cursor to the next cell, ESCAPE can be used to cancel the last command before the ENTER is pressed. Some special keys and their purpose are shown in Figure 3.7.

Special keys can be combined with ordinary keys to carry out a range of very powerful actions. These are called 'keyboard shortcuts' – for example, to save a copy of a document, press Ctrl key and 'S'.

What does a function key do?

Some keyboards have 'function' keys which are assigned special functions by software. For example, pressing F1 may bring up the Help screen. When used in conjunction with other keys, such as ALT and SHIFT the key may perform a different function.

Your turn

1 Which keys on the keyboard are shaped differently from the letter keys? Why are these keys often larger than the letter keys?
2 What is the purpose of the special keys on your keyboard? Choose a piece of software familiar to you and see if you can do the following using special keys:

◆ open a file ◆ print a file ◆ save a file ◆ quit a file.

3 Make a list of the keyboard shortcuts that you use for particular pieces of software.
4 Try moving between different applications in Windows using key combinations such as the 'toggle' ALT and TAB.

Ergonomics of the keyboard

Ergonomics of the keyboard refers to:

- the size and position of a key
- the shape of a key
- the curve of the face of a key
- the noise a key makes when it is depressed
- the angle of the keyboard

- the tactile response of keyboard – that is, the finger pressure required to register the key being depressed and the distance the key moves when it is pressed.

Laptop and notebook computers have a built-in keyboard and mouse or tracker ball. When buying a computer, you should examine and 'test drive' the keyboard.

Methods of operating a keyboard

Touch-typing

Touch-typing is using the keyboard with all fingers and the right thumb without looking at the keys. With practice, both the finger to use and the reach required to strike the key will become second nature and so it is possible to type without consciously thinking about where the keys are.

What are the advantages of being able to touch-type?

The advantages of being able to touch-type are:

- attention can be directed to what is being keyed rather than where the keys are

- a keyboard operator can type in the range of 40 to 80 words per minute compared to handwriting speeds for most people of 20 to 25 words per minute.

Home row keys

With touch-typing the fingers have 'home' positions on the keyboard. The fingers always return to these positions after pressing a key. With the fingers on the home row keys you can see G and H between the hands. Some keyboards have a raised 'dot' which is easy to feel on a left (D or F) and right (J or K) home row key as a guide, to make sure the correct finger is on the correct key. Figure 3.8 shows the position of the home fingers in relation to the basic keyboard as well as giving the name of the home finger.

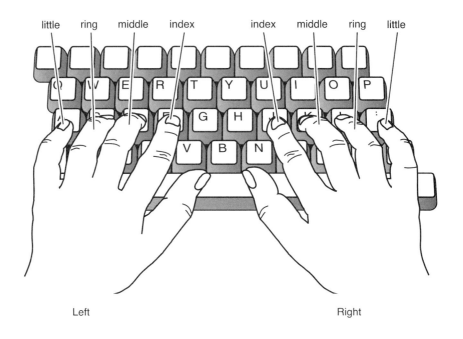

Figure 3.8   Home row position for fingers

The space bar is operated by the thumb of the right hand. Figure 3.9 shows how each finger is allocated a group of keys. Some fingers, such as the F finger, have responsibility for eight keys, others, such as the D finger, have four keys. The little fingers have responsibility for special keys, such as SHIFT, TAB and ENTER.

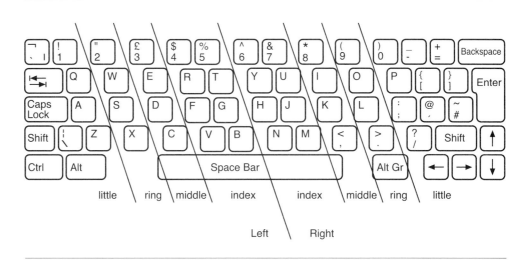

Figure 3.9   Allocation of fingers to keys on the QWERTY keyboard

Your turn

1 If your keyboard has raised dots, on which letter keys are they located? Gently place your fingers on these keys and feel the dot with your fingers. Be conscious of the dots when resting your fingers on the home row keys.
2 Which keys on the keyboard are struck with the 'A' finger?
3 Which hand and which finger of that hand are responsible for the following:

- letter U
- number 8

- full stop
- letter T

- letter O
- symbol %

What does learning to touch-type involve?

A person can become skilled in the use of the keyboard with about fifteen hours of continuous instruction and training. Keyboarding is a manual skill and needs practice to show progress. In the early stages, regular sessions over a short period of time are of most benefit. These sessions will consist mainly of:

- warm up drills and review of keys already learnt

- introduction to new keys
- short exercises to practice new keys.

Beginners generally have to overcome a few problem areas. Table 3.2 lists some of these problems.

Table 3.2   Problems usually encountered by the touch-typing beginner

Problem	Advice
Keys struck with the little fingers such as A, Q and ENTER seem very difficult.	The little fingers are usually the weakest; they will develop strength.
Some reaches seem too far – for example, keys on the upper row, such as the number 1.	At first, the fingers may seem a little short to reach the upper row, it is a matter of practice and the fingers will soon become used to stretching the distance.
The apparent slowing down in keystroking speed when a two-finger typist learns to touch-type.	This is only short term; very soon, speeds far in excess of two-finger typing will be achieved.
Co-ordination to type upper case characters using the SHIFT keys, which requires the little finger on one hand and the keying finger on the other to work together, is hard to achieve.	Use of the SHIFT keys to type capital letters does require some practice and co-ordination. If this is a weak area then spend time on those drills which improve this area of technique.
Striking the keys with too much force. Some beginners become frustrated looking for a key, then 'dive bomb' and bash the key when they find it.	Press the key only with enough force to register the character; it requires less energy and is much quicker. Develop the skill of using as little pressure as possible.

Health and safety issues related to computer use

Occupational overuse syndrome

There has been much research into the effect of posture and technique on keyboarding, particularly in regard to 'occupational overuse syndrome'. This syndrome is also referred to as RSI (repetition strain injury). If a keyboard is used to enter information at high speed for long periods of time without breaks there is a danger of injury being suffered. Occupational overuse syndrome covers a range of pains and discomforts associated with the soft tissue, tendon and muscles.

Your turn

1 Use a word processor and key in the following text. (Aim to reduce the pressure required to operate the keys to the bare minimum.)

> For this exercise strike the keys on the keyboard as lightly as possible. Listen to the sound that is made by the keys when you are striking them. The less noise the better. Try striking the keys with your eyes closed and listen to the noise the keys make when struck. Strike the keys with firm pressure but not with great force.

2 What did you notice about the finger pressure required to activate the keys? Would this make a difference if you were using a keyboard for an extended period of time?

Keyboarding posture and technique

Posture is how you place your body. Correct posture can mean tiring less easily and preventing undue stress on your body. Being relaxed when using a keyboard means working more effectively. Get into the habit of adopting good posture and correct keyboarding technique at the start of each keyboarding session. Figure 3.10 shows correct posture when seated at a keyboard, and Table 3.3 details how to sit on the chair correctly.

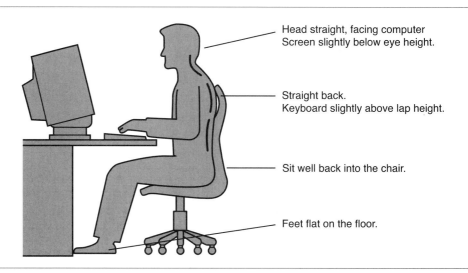

Head straight, facing computer
Screen slightly below eye height.

Straight back.
Keyboard slightly above lap height.

Sit well back into the chair.

Feet flat on the floor.

Figure 3.10   Correct seating at a keyboard

Posture and technique can be divided into two main areas:

- how to sit on the chair and address the keyboard and screen
- the position of arms, hands and fingers on the keyboard and the technique for pressing the keys.

Table 3.3   How to sit on the chair

Feet	Should be flat on the floor, about two shoe widths' apart
Seat	Your weight is transferred down the back evenly to the seat
Back	Reasonably upright without being stiff
Shoulders	Relaxed without dropping or being stiff
Head	Held up in line with the body – not forward of the body line

The position of the arms and fingering technique are:

- arms – hanging along the side of the body, forearms should be parallel to the floor and line of the thighs
- wrists – should be straight, parallel to the floor and line of the thighs. If necessary the hands can be slightly higher than the elbows (within 0 to 20 degrees above horizontal)
- fingers – relaxed with a gentle curve
- position of fingers to keyboard – fingers should be almost 180 degrees to the keyboard.

Quickly glance at the keyboard and check the position of your fingers before your start: you should see the 'G' and 'H' keys in the space between your fingers. Other factors that contribute to a healthy and safe learning and working environment when using a computer include:

- desk design – Computer desks have adjustable heights for working areas – for example, the keyboard. The mouse should be the same height as the keyboard.
- desk height – A keyboard height in the range of 58 to 71 centimetres is considered suitable for most users.
- chair design – The seat height and back support should be adjustable.
- seat height – The height should be adjustable so the feet rest flat on the floor, and the hands address the keyboard correctly.
- screen height – The top of the screen should be at or slightly below eye height.
- screen distance – In the range 45 to 71 centimetres is satisfactory. If the monitor has controls for brightness and contrast these may need adjustment.

Work area and practices

When sitting at a desk make sure that the things you need are within easy reach. If you are keying in large amounts of information it is important that you take rest periods away from the computer and fit VDU filters.

Your turn

1 Describe the environment in which you use a computer. Mention factors such as the furniture, desks, chairs, lighting and workspace. How easy is it to work in this environment?
2 What type of ergonomic aids do you use when working at a computer?

Keyboarding software and learning to touch-type

Software which assists in the teaching and improvement of touch-typing keyboard skills is classified as a 'typing tutor' e.g. 'Mavis Beacon'. There are many books devoted to keyboarding instruction and development of touch-typing skills. Keyboarding software typically:

- allows the user to set targets for the amount of practice each session
- allows the user to set goal levels of speed and accuracy
- sets the level of difficulty of the exercises
- advises on recommended drills to overcome problem areas (for example, practice the upper row keys)
- provides tests of differing time length and degree of difficulty.

The analysis provided by the software usually includes:

- comparison of actual practice time with desired practice goal
- instant speed and error analysis showing individual fingers and separate characters
- speed and accuracy figures, expressed in terms of number of words typed per minute with percentage accuracy. Figure 3.11 shows speed and accuracy by letter group.

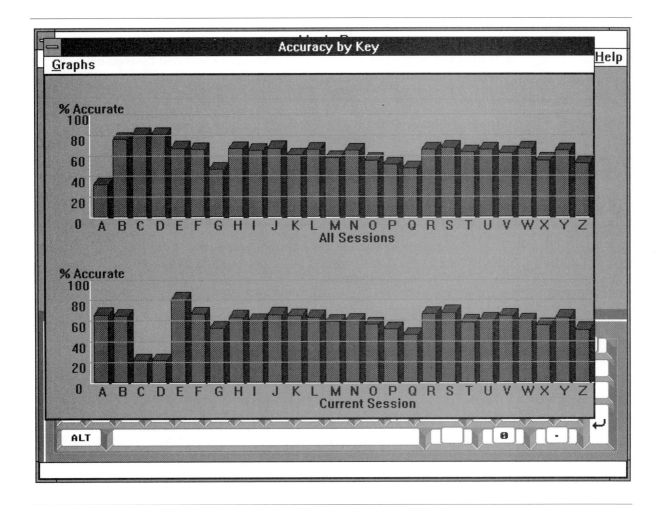

Figure 3.11   Extract of screen display from 'Mavis Beacon' software (accuracy by letter)

Lessons	Keyboard	Style
Keys & Fingers		**F3**
Free Typing		F4
Do a Game Instead		F11
Custom Lesson...		
Take 10-Key Lessons		F10
Pause Lesson		F2
Quit Lesson		

Figure 3.12   Example of keyboard lesson menu

With 'Mavis Beacon' the user selects appropriate exercises from the Lesson menu to improve his or her level of skill. Figure 3.12 shows the Lesson menu for this program. Other keyboarding software offers similar features.

Your turn

1 What does Figure 3.11 tell you about the user's overall skill level?
2 Which letters are the best and the weakest as identified by Figure 3.11 in terms of accuracy?
3 Which letters have become weaker during the current session?
4 Imagine you are using keyboarding software which has selections like those in the menu in Figure 3.12. Which menu item would you select to improve:
   ◆ using your middle fingers?
   ◆ typing the numbers '4', '7' and the £ symbol?
   ◆ set up a lesson for improving typing letters 'C', 'V' and 'B'.

Numeric keypad

The numeric keypad is found on the right-hand side of the keyboard. The numbers are in the same position for all keypads. A numeric keypad is useful if a lot of numbers are to be entered. The keypad is operated with the right hand and fingers of the right hand are allocated a column of keys as shown in Figure 3.13.

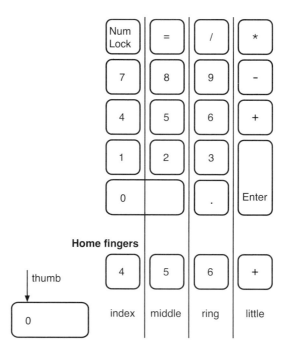

Figure 3.13   Allocation of keys on a numeric keypad

Handwriting and voice

Pen computers allow limited input of data in hand-written form. Voice recognition is also becoming available for use with personal computers. In the immediate future, however, the keyboard will be the dominant form of input for computers.

Your turn

1 Do you think the keyboard will be replaced entirely by other methods of input?
2 List the programs you have used that do not rely solely on keyboard input.
3 Name another peripheral that can be used to input text directly.
4 Keep a file of articles about alternative input methods such as touch screens, voice recognition, and handwriting tablets.
5 How do you think these methods of input compare with the use of the keyboard?
6 What are the things that need to be overcome before these alternative methods become more common?

Review questions

1 What different types of keys are found on a computer keyboard?
2 Explain the purpose and function of CAPS LOCK and SHIFT.
3 Why are sentences typed in capital letters difficult to read?
4 Why is correct posture important when using a keyboard?
5 What space should normally be left after a punctuation mark?
6 How can keyboards be different in terms of ergonomics?

Tasks

1 The following keys may be on your keyboard. See if you can find the following keys: CONTROL, ALT, COMMAND, ESCAPE, PAGE UP, PAGE DOWN, HOME, END, function keys, NUMLOCK, SCROLL, PAUSE, BREAK, PRINT SCREEN, INSERT.

2 Interview a person who spends his or her working time mainly using a computer. Find out how importantly this person rates health and safety issues. Does he or she vary activities so as to prevent spending too long a period keying in information?

3 Describe the keyboard you are using. The following points may provide a guide:

- name and make of the keyboard
- whether or not the manufacturer of the keyboard is different from that of the computer
- how the keys feel when they are struck
- the size and shape of the keyboard
- whether or not the angle of the keyboard can be adjusted
- whether or not the keyboard has raised dots to help fingers locate the keys by touch.

Find another keyboard and prepare a comparison report. If possible, find a keyboard produced by another manufacturer.

4 Examine a keyboard for a laptop computer and a desktop computer. What are the main differences between the keyboards regarding:

- size of the keyboard
- size of the keys
- number of keys
- the ease at which the angle of the keyboard can be adjusted
- the support given to the wrists.

Which keyboard do you think is easier to operate?

Word processing

4

What is a word processor?

A word processor is a piece of computer software that deals with text-based material. It is possible to create a new document, then edit and change the text in the document. The document can be stored on disk, retrieved from the disk, formatted and then printed.

Word-processed text in a file is often referred to as a document. Using a word processor makes it easier to organise ideas as the text can be altered easily.

The work on disk (files) can be changed and formatted in many ways before printing (the material that is printed out is called 'hard copy').

 Your turn

1 What is the name of the word processing software that you use at: home; school, elsewhere?
2 What do you use this software for?

What are the main features of word processors?

A word processor will typically consist of the application, a dictionary (for the spelling checker), a thesaurus, a help file and templates.

Most word processors can:

- automatically move the cursor to the next line when the end of a line is reached (called 'word wrap')
- format the document in various text fonts and styles
- move text into a new position (cut and paste)
- copy text and place it in a document any number of times (copy and paste)
- link to a spelling checker
- align text to the left or right margin or the centre of the page
- set margins for a document
- divide the document into separate pages for printing
- show the whole page on screen in a reduced view (called 'page preview')
- automatically number pages
- find where a character or word occurs in a document
- change a character, word or group of words in a document
- provide on-line help
- offer choices for words by linking to a thesaurus
- import information/graphics from other applications.

The word processor screen display

When you open the word processor to create a new document the screen will most likely show:

◆ a menu bar at the top of the screen

◆ a window for the document.

Figure 4.1 shows part of the screen for the WORD 6 word processor with a document in progress.

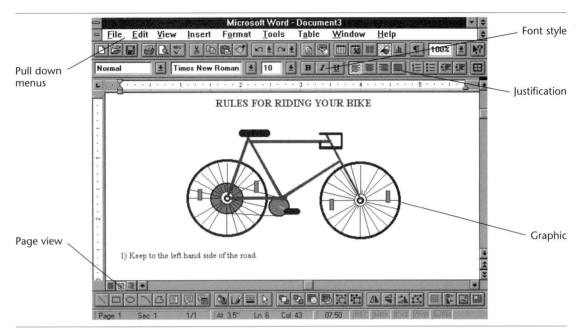

Pull down menus

Font style

Justification

Page view

Graphic

Figure 4.1 WORD 6 word processor screen

Your turn

How does your word processor screen display compare with Figure 4.1? Make a list of similarities and differences.

Writing using the word processor

When starting a new document treat the computer screen like a blank sheet of paper on which the main points are to be written. Just enter the main points as a list on screen, pressing ENTER (RETURN) between each idea. There is no need to form sentences or paragraphs.

Your turn

1 This exercise requires you to compose text using the keyboard. Topic: What I like doing best.
   a Make a list of the five main points (single words only) you want to include. Give the document a name and save the document, using Save As.
   b Form the list into an order.
   c Form the words into sentences.
   d Form the sentences in paragraphs.
   e 'Save' the edited version of the document.
2 Write some text by hand. Then enter it on the word processor.
3 Describe how entering text from hand-written copy is different from entering typewritten copy.

How and when should document files be saved?

Documents need to be saved regularly. Save after important changes have been made. At the end of a session a backup copy should be made. Always allow enough time at the end of a session to make sure that you are not in a hurry when saving your documents.

Some word processors can be set automatically to save documents at a regular interval – for example, every five minutes. When a document is saved it is a good idea to give it a name which is related to its contents. Most filenames are limited to 8 characters – for example, a filename could include the authors initials, an abbreviation of the file content, and the version of the document (e.g. RDALET1).

Steps to document creation

Figure 4.2 shows the basis processes in document creation.

Figure 4.2 Steps in word processing a document

Your turn

Why is 'saving' the document the most important step in the creation of a document? List two other important steps.

What is the cursor?

A cursor is a point of light which appears on the computer screen. The on-screen cursor shows the current active position of the word processor. The cursor will flash to make it easier to locate on the screen.

The cursor shape

There are a variety of ways in which the cursor will appear on screen. It could appear as:

- a square
- a flashing vertical line
- an underline bar.

If the cursor changes shape then this may indicate a change in the function that can be performed. For example, if the cursor becomes:

- an 'I' beam   I   the cursor has moved from the current insertion point
- an arrow   the cursor has moved from the current insertion point in the scroll bar, it is used to scroll through a document, or to pull down a menu.

Your turn

1 What is the shape of the cursor on your word processor?
2 Does the shape of the cursor change when it is moved around the screen? If so, how?

How can the cursor be used to insert text?

Place the cursor immediately to the left of where the next character will be entered and press a character key on the keyboard.

Word wrap

Word processor 'word wrap'. When a line is full, words are moved automatically to the next line. It is only necessary to press the ENTER key at the end of a paragraph. Word wrap is most useful if the document is to be re-formatted later (for example, to change the margins). The line length will automatically fit the new margins.

Your turn

1 Enter the following line of text. Do not press the ENTER key at any stage.

> The best thing about the holiday was the weather. It was terrific every day. The sun was shining through the early morning mist and the wind was very light.

2 At what point did the text run on to the next line?

How can the cursor be used to delete a single character?

If the cursor is a vertical line, place it to the right of the character to be deleted and press the DELETE key.

Your turn

1 Type the line as it appears below. Then make the changes to the line as shown by the arrows.

Insert letter 'a'

During our time away we red books, ate ice-creams and slept in eachmorning. It was great fun.

Insert space

2 Save a copy of the document. Call the document by your given name and add Ex after it – for example, if you name is BEN you would name the document 'BENEX'.

Selecting and deleting a block of text

If text is to be edited it has to be 'selected'. To select text place the cursor at the start of the text then:

◆ with the mouse button down 'drag' the cursor to the end of the text to be selected.

Selected text shows as reversed on the screen. For example, the following line has been selected:

> Selected text shows as inverse on the screen.

To delete a block, select the block of text and use the DELETE key.

Your turn

Select the text which was entered in the previous 'Your turn' and delete it. Close the file but do not save the changes you have just made. Open the file again to make sure that it is intact.

What are cut, copy and paste?

Text can be moved around in a document after it has been entered. To 'cut and paste' means to move the text from one position to a new position. To 'copy and paste' means to make a copy of the original text and paste the copy somewhere else in the document.

How is text moved using 'cut and paste'?

Selected text can be cut from a position and pasted elsewhere in the document. Table 4.1 shows the steps involved.

Most word processors have a cut icon and a paste icon . Alternatively these commands can be found under the Edit menu.

Table 4.1   How to cut and paste

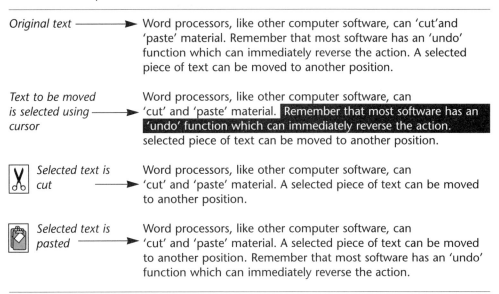

Original text	Word processors, like other computer software, can 'cut'and 'paste' material. Remember that most software has an 'undo' function which can immediately reverse the action. A selected piece of text can be moved to another position.
Text to be moved is selected using cursor	Word processors, like other computer software, can 'cut' and 'paste' material. Remember that most software has an 'undo' function which can immediately reverse the action. selected piece of text can be moved to another position.
Selected text is cut	Word processors, like other computer software, can 'cut' and 'paste' material. A selected piece of text can be moved to another position.
Selected text is pasted	Word processors, like other computer software, can 'cut' and 'paste' material. A selected piece of text can be moved to another position. Remember that most software has an 'undo' function which can immediately reverse the action.

Your turn

1 Enter the text in the paragraph called 'Original text' in Table 4.1.
2 Using cut and paste, change the paragraph to the same as paragraph called 'Selected text is pasted'.

How is text copied using 'copy and paste'?

Copy and paste can be very useful to transfer text from one document to another. Figure 4.3 shows text that has been copied and pasted.

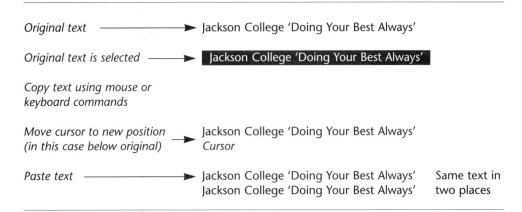

Original text	Jackson College 'Doing Your Best Always'
Original text is selected	Jackson College 'Doing Your Best Always'
Copy text using mouse or keyboard commands	
Move cursor to new position (in this case below original)	Jackson College 'Doing Your Best Always' Cursor
Paste text	Jackson College 'Doing Your Best Always' Same text in Jackson College 'Doing Your Best Always' two places

Figure 4.3   Steps to 'copy and paste'

Your turn

1 Carry out the exercise shown in Figure 4.3. Paste the text into the document three times.
2 How do you select the following on the word processor you are using: a character; a word; a line; a paragraph; a document?
3 What is the difference between 'cut and paste' and 'copy and paste'?

4 This exercise can be done if your word processor allows more than one document to be open at the same time.
   a Open two documents that you have created.
   b Select a paragraph of text from one document. Copy the text.
   c Open the other document and paste the information into it.

Moving through a document

You can move around a document by using:

- a mouse
- the arrow keys
- END and HOME keys
- the scroll bars (called scrolling through a document)
- PAGE UP or PAGE DOWN keys
- function keys.

   The 'Find' command can be used to go to a particular piece of text, usually a word. The 'Go To' command can be used to go to a particular page.

Your turn

1 Complete each task before moving on to the next. Save the document at least at the end of each step.
   a Call the document 'holiday' and include your name or initials in the document name.
   b List the places you would like to go for a holiday. Press ENTER at the end of each place to move to a new paragraph.
   c List the places in order of preference. Use cut and paste to reorder them.
   d Next to each place, provide a one sentence reason saying why you would like to go there. The reason is to be contained in the same paragraph.
   e After you have entered the reasons, check the order of places. Use cut and paste if you wish to change the order again.
   f Print a copy of the document.
   g Copy the material for the first five choices, create a new document and copy the material to the new document. Save the new document.
2 Refer to your word processing manual or on-line help and write down how you can move the cursor to the beginning and end of a: word; line; sentence; paragraph; screen; page; document.
3 Key in the following line:

   This is line number

   a Copy the line.
   b Paste the line into the document three times. There should now be four lines.
   c Add numbers to the end of each line so that they appear as below:

   This is line number 3
   This is line number 4
   This is line number 2
   This is line number 1

   d Using cut and paste, select the lines and put the lines in the correct order, from 1 to 4. How many cut and pastes does it take to do this?

Entering text with a word processor

Text first, format later

With a word processor the text can be entered and altered until the content and the layout is satisfactory. Generally it is best to enter the text and format the document later.

Devote time and attention to keying in your ideas first, pay less attention to typing errors as they can be corrected later.

Key points

The standard rules for entering text on a word processor are:

- Only press the ENTER key at the end of a paragraph. Let 'word wrap' put words onto the next line within a paragraph.
- Leave only one space after a full stop.
- Do not use a hyphen unless it is part of a name.
- Do not use the space bar apart from inserting a single space – do not use it to format text.
- Check the upper case or SHIFT key setting. Ordinary text should be entered in lower case, capital letters in upper case.

Referring to text in a document

Text can be referred to as a character, word, line, sentence, paragraph or page.

What is a character?

A single key pressed on the keyboard will produce a character:

- a lower case letter of the alphabet – for example, **a**, **b**
- a number – for example, **7**, **9**
- a punctuation symbol – for example, **?**, **"**
- a symbol – for example, **&**, *****, **®**.

What is a word?

A word is a character or group of characters, which have meaning, joined together with a space either side. For example, 'a' and 'this' are both words.

What is a sentence?

A sentence is a group of words which make complete sense on its own. A sentence starts with a capital letter and is completed by a full stop.

What is a line?

A line is made of characters placed together on a row between the left and right margins. A line can be part of a sentence, part of a paragraph or a separate paragraph.

What is a paragraph?

A paragraph is usually defined as a group of sentences followed by an 'enter' character at a point where it is logical to have a slight break. The 'enter' forces the insert point to the left margin on the next line. This type of 'enter' is also referred to as a 'hard return'. Therefore, a paragraph could be just a single line followed by a return character. The ¶ character often signifies this 'hard' return. For example, the line shown in Figure 4.4 shows the line of text and a paragraph marker. Find out how to show the paragraph character and other non-printing characters on your word processor.

Line of text → This is a paragraph. ¶ ← Paragraph marker

Figure 4.4   An example of a paragraph in a word processor

What is 'WYSIWYG'?

Many word processors show on screen what the document will look like when it is printed. This is referred to as 'what you see is what you get' (WYSIWYG), pronounced 'wizzy-wig'. It is called print preview.

Page layout

It is important to check the paper size so that the document can be set with correct margins. For example, a standard paper size is A4. A4 paper is 210mm wide by 297mm long. The margins are the blank spaces surrounding the sides of the page. Another common page size is US letter (United States letter). US letter size is 8.5 inches (216mm) wide by 11.00 inches (279mm) long. Figure 4.5 shows the parts of a page.

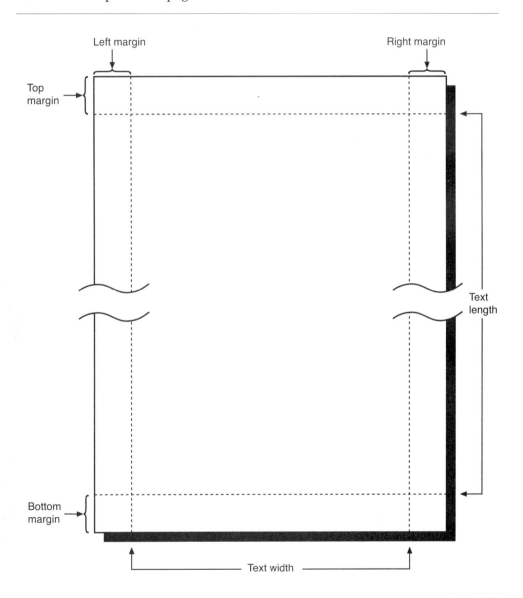

Figure 4.5 Reduced page view showing margins

Setting up your document

Word processors have 'default' settings. A default setting is a value the software uses for a setting until it is changed by the user.

A word processor may open with default settings for:

- screen font and size
- page size
- measurement unit for ruler
- margins
- page number
- printer.

What on-screen information is provided by a word processor?

A word processor provides on-screen information about the document and the current settings. For example:

- position and types of tabs
- margins
- page width
- line spacing
- justification of the lines (alignment of a line to the left or right margin or to the centre of the page).

The settings above would normally be set using the ruler.

The ruler

The ruler shows the current settings for the document. Figure 4.6 shows an example of a ruler with left and right margin settings.

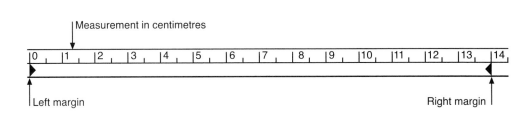

Figure 4.6 Example of a word processor ruler

A new ruler can be placed in a document if the margins need to be changed. For example, the first page may be a title page requiring different margins from the main part of the document. Altered ruler settings apply to selected text or text below the current ruler.

Page centring (horizontal and vertical)

As a general rule it is a good idea to have the left and right margins of equal width and the top and bottom margins of equal depth. This means that the page will be horizontally and vertically centred on the paper when printed. A centred page looks balanced whereas unequal margins tend to distract the reader.

Your turn

1 List the default Page Layout settings of the word processor you are using.
2 What settings do you prefer for the word processor? Why do you prefer these settings?

Editing a document

When a document is in its final stages it needs to be carefully checked and re-drafted. Editing involves checking:

- spelling
- grammar
- punctuation
- paragraph organisation
- position of the page breaks in the document (called pagination).

Editing on screen

It can be difficult to get the feel of a document when re-drafting on-screen. Documents should be edited on-screen as much as possible before printing out. However, it is unlikely that all errors will be found by on-screen editing.

What does a spelling checker do?

If a word in a document is incorrectly keyed in or incorrectly spelt it may be found by using a spelling checker. Some dictionaries are based on American spellings, although others are British. For example:

British dictionary
- colour
- centring
- defence

American dictionary
- color
- centering
- defense

A dictionary usually has two parts: the main dictionary and a user dictionary. The main dictionary cannot usually be changed by a user; however, a word used on a regular basis but not recognised by the main dictionary can be put into the user dictionary. Names of people and place-names do not usually appear in a dictionary and would need to be included in a user dictionary.

Figure 4.7 (on page 48) shows the spelling checker window for the Microsoft Word word processor. A spelling checker can:

- find a word that it considers is spelt incorrectly
- suggest alternatives for the word
- add words to the user dictionary
- replace the word with the correctly spelt word.

What are the limitations of spelling checkers?

Examine the spelling checker that comes with the word processor because:

- the quality of dictionaries can vary
- if a word is spelt incorrectly but used in the wrong context it will not be detected, for example, 'their' and 'there'
- names of people and places are usually not included
- the same two words in a row may not be detected, for example, 'the the'.

When using a word it may still be necessary to check a printed dictionary to make sure that you are using the word correctly.

Figure 4.7 Spelling checker for Microsoft Word

Your turn

For the following exercise, check your answers with a partner.

1 Each of following sentences contains an error that would not be picked up by a spelling checker. Find the error.

- The boat was tied to a boy.
- Wear is the pencil?
- The car is parked over their.
- The plain flew in the air.

2 Give four examples of other incorrectly spelt words that the spelling checker would not pick up.

3 Key your family name into a document and apply the spelling checker. What is the result? Can you add your name to the dictionary? If so, how?

4 Does the dictionary for the word processor you are using have a name? Is it British or American? How many words are in the dictionary?

5 Are the following words contained in the dictionary you are using: user-friendly; AIDS; coursework; monitoring; yuppie?

6 Suggest and find words that are relatively new to the language but not included in the word processor dictionary.

How should hard copy be edited?

A draft copy of the document needs to be edited carefully to pick up errors. There are standard proof-reading marks used to show the error and its correction. The original error and the correction mark should still be clear, as the text may yet be left as it was originally.

Your turn

1 How many meanings do the following words have in your printed dictionary: set, run, go, open, strike, school, self? What do you think are the three most common uses of each word?

2 Find the meaning of 'green' in your dictionary. Does the dictionary meaning reflect the different meanings the word can have today?

3 Does the term 'user-friendly' appear in your dictionary? What does the term mean? Give an example of how you would use the term.

Formatting a document

The final stage of document creation is formatting – that is, deciding how a document looks. A range of fonts and settings can be tried before a document is completed.

Formatting refers to the way in which a document is arranged and is determined by the:

- justification of lines
- amount of space between paragraphs
- use of fully blocked or indented paragraphs
- use of fonts and font styles.

Tips for consistent document formatting

The following will assist in formatting a document:

- if you use headings and sub-headings, make sure that they are consistent
- try to keep to one or two fonts throughout, using bold and italic as variations
- use consistent line spacing throughout the text. Spacing can be changed to single spacing, line and a half, double or other spacing later.

Justification of lines and paragraphs

◆ Left justified – each line will start on the left-hand margin. This is a default style for most word processors and will leave a ragged right margin:

This text is left justified.
This test is left justified. This text is left justified.
This text is left justified. This text is left justified. This text is left justified.

◆ Right justified – each line will finish on the right-hand margin. You may use this to give a story a dramatic effect on a particular line or lines. This style will produce a ragged left margin:

This text is right justified.
This text is right justified. This text is right justified.
This text is right justified. This text is right justified. This text is right justified.

◆ Centred – each line will be placed an equal distance from the left and right-hand margins. If the left and right margins are the same, the line will be in the centre of the page. This style is often selected for heading so that they stand out:

This text is centred.
This text is centred. This text is centred.
This text is centred. This text is centred. This text is centred.

◆ Fully justified – each line will start on the left-hand margin and finish on the right-hand margin. The spacing between the words is altered to ensure that this occurs:

This text is fully justified. This text is fully justified. This text is fully justified. This text is fully justified. This text is fully justified. This text is fully justified. This text is fully justified. This text is fully justified.

Your turn

Key in the following line:

Big Ben, the bell that strikes the hour in the Great Clock of Westminster, weighs 13.5 tons and is cracked.

 a Copy and paste the line into the document three times.
 b Format the first line as left justified.
 c Format the second line as right justified.
 d Format the third line as centred.
 e Format the fourth line as fully justified.
 f Compare your results with the lines below.

Big Ben, the bell that strikes the hour in the Great Clock of Westminster, weighs 13.5 tons and is cracked.

Big Ben, the bell that strikes the hour in the Great Clock of Westminster, weighs 13.5 tons and is cracked.

Big Ben, the bell that strikes the hour in the Great Clock of Westminster, weighs 13.5 tons and is cracked.

What is a font?

A font refers to the shape and style of the typeface that is used to represent characters. Each font is given a name that refers to the family of letters with that design. Many of the popular fonts have been used in the printing industry for hundreds of years.

It's either a tin chicken, an intergalactic monster or a rampaging font

Most word processors are able to display a range of fonts on the screen. The size of a font is referred to in 'points'. A point is a printing industry measure; one point equals 1/72 inch.

The font to be used in a document should be chosen so that it helps to make the document legible. There are two main options for typefaces: serif and sans serif. Serif fonts have additional strokes like small tails at the ends of the characters. The following are examples of three serif fonts (each is set in 18 point):

Times New Roman   Caxton   Courier

Sans serif fonts do not have these finishing strokes. The following are examples of three sans serif fonts (each is set in 18 point):

Helvetica   Arial   Geometric

This is how the main characters of the popular serif font 'Times New Roman' look:

abcdefghijklmnopqrstuvwxyz 0123456789

This is how the main characters of the popular sans serif font 'Helvetica' look:

abcdefghijklmnopqrstuvwxyz 0123456789

Your turn

1 The letter k is shown below in lower and upper case in the Times New Roman and Helvetica fonts. What are the differences?

k   k   K   K

Times New Roman Helvetica   Times New Roman Helvetica

2 The following are examples of different fonts. What differences can you see between them?

Times New Roman Arial
Humanist   New York

3 Do you like using different types of fonts? Why? List three fonts you like using.

Variation in font size and style

Many word processors offer variations in font size and style. Figure 4.8 shows the alternatives available for each font in the Microsoft Word word processing software.

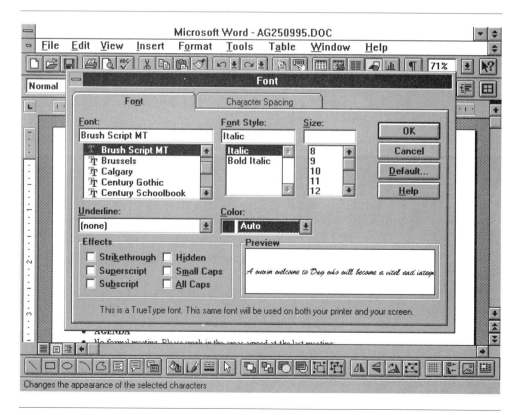

Figure 4.8 Variations in font size and style in Microsoft Word

Varying font sizes can make headings stand out. The size of a heading can be set according to its importance. An important heading would usually be in a larger font size. Normal text font size is 10 or 12 point. Text in a range of point sizes follows:

This is Times New Roman in 9 point size

This is Times New Roman in 10 point size

This is Times New Roman in 12 point size

This is Times New Roman in 14 point size

This is Times New Roman in 18 point size

Times New Roman in 24 point

Variations of font style

Table 4.2 shows the variations in font characteristics offered by word processors.

Table 4.2   Variations in font characters

Feature	Example	Use
Plain	This text is plain	The default setting – this can be altered by the user.
Bold	**This text is bold.**	Use for headings and important words in a document.
Italic	*This text is italic.*	Use for emphasis on words in a document.
<u>Underline</u>	<u>This text is underlined.</u>	Be careful with the use of underline as some letters such as y, g and j, which descend below the line, may be cut through by the underline.
Outline	This text is outlined	Use only in special cases, as it is difficult to read for large amounts of text.
Shadow	This text is shadowed.	Use only in special cases, as it is difficult to read for large amounts of text.

Combining font styles

Some of the font styles can be combined, such as:

This text is in bold italic.

<u>This text is in bold underline.</u>

Bold, italic and underline are used regularly. Outline and shadow are not easy to read and should be used only for special purposes. They should not appear in a document that contains a large amount of text. It is difficult to distinguish the letters in the following line, which is in an outline font:

The use of computers in word processing

Your turn

Key in the following text. Select the line and format it in a font that has a 12 point size.

> My favourite dessert is vanilla ice-cream covered in chocolate and nuts.

a Copy the line and paste it back into the document to make three lines.
b Leave the first line formatted as plain text.
c Format the second line in bold.
d Format the third line in italics.
e Compare your screen display with the examples below:

> My favourite dessert is vanilla ice-cream covered in chocolate and nuts.
>
> **My favourite dessert is vanilla ice-cream covered in chocolate and nuts.**
>
> *My favourite dessert is vanilla ice-cream covered in chocolate and nu*ts.

What is a tab?

When the TAB key is pressed once, the cursor will move to a pre-set position on that line. Tabs are useful when setting out tables and figures in a document.

The word processor will have a default setting for:

◆ the position of the tabs – for example, it may be every 1.27cm

◆ the type of tab (the normal default setting for a tab type is left).

How is a tab set?

A tab can be set by:

◆ selecting the tab icon and dragging it onto the ruler in the appropriate position

◆ entering a value in a dialogue box.

Word processors allow the tabs to be altered after the text has been entered; if a tab is reset the selected text will move to the new position.

How is tab setting changed?

Figure 4.9 shows how to change the setting. The tab which applies to the selected text will cause the text to move to the new position.

   When keying in a table, work across each line, press return to move down to the next line. To alter the alignment select the text and alter the tab setting.

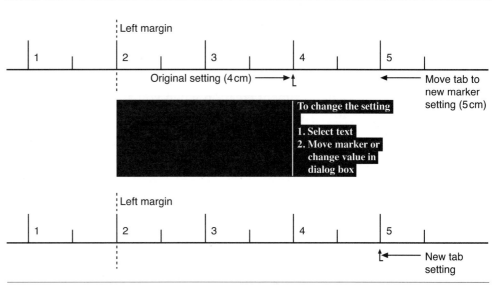

Figure 4.9   Resetting a tab

Your turn

The following table shows the area and population of each country in the United Kingdom. The area column has been set with a right justified tab, the percentage column has been set with a decimal tab.

United Kingdom: area in square kilometres and population in '000s by constituent countries:

Country	Population '000s	%	Area sq. km.	%
England	48,208	83.4	130,423	53.9
Scotland	5,107	8.8	77,080	31.9
Wales	2,891	5.0	20,766	8.6
Northern Ireland	1,594	2.8	13,483	5.6
United Kingdom (total)	57,800	100.0	241,752	100.00

Printing a document

Check that the word processor is set up for the printer before printing.

Print preview

Most word processors enable you to see how each page will look before it is printed. This view is a reduced size view. It gives an overall view of the page. Figure 4.5 on page 45 is an example of how the print preview may appear on screen.

Draft copy

Many printers have a setting called 'draft', which allows the document to be printed out more quickly than normal. Draft quality is useful in the early stage of document creation when you are more concerned about the text than the formatting.

Printout of final copy

Printing a document at best quality is carried out at the end of the document's creation. Page breaks and formatting may be changed at this stage and these can be checked on screen before printing the final copy.

Your turn

Keep a draft copy and a final copy printout of a document you have printed. What are the differences regarding the time taken to print the document, and the printing quality?

Active windows

Sound and video documents can be included in a word processed document. Figure 4.10 shows a QuickTime movie and a sound button included as part of the document. Double clicking on the movie plays the movie, double clicking on the sound button will play the stored sound.

A person could be quoted in the text of a document and with the audio recorded it would be possible to hear them speaking or the National song of Ireland could be played.

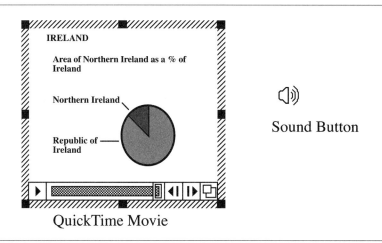

QuickTime Movie

Figure 4.10   Microsoft Works document with QuickTime and Sound included

What identifying information should be included in an assignment?

When submitting an assignment the following details should be included.

- date
- school name
- student's name
- student year level
- subject
- teacher
- the nature of the task e.g., homework, coursework
- the specific task or question
- due date.

An example of this type of information and how it could be set out appears in Figure 4.11.

Information:

Seaview Comprehensive School
Name: Jaspal Gill
Tutor Group: 9YGT
Keystage 3 – English

Homework: Newspaper article based on book character
Date: 21 March 1996
Due: 28 March 1996

Seaview Comprehensive School

School name
24 point
bold
centred

'Newspaper article based on imaginary interview with character in a book of my choice'

Topic
18 point
bold
centred

Details
12 point
range
left

English Homework
Set: 21 March 1996
Due: 28 March 1996

Jaspal Gill: 9YGT
Key Stage: 3
Teacher: Mrs. Honey

Details
12 point
range
right

Figure 4.11   Layout for an assignment

Your turn

1 What information would you record for an assignment you currently have to complete?

2 Set out the details in Figure 4.11 differently. For example, key information – such as name – could be in a bold font. The title could be on a separate line. Compare your layout with the example in Figure 4.11.

Tips for setting out paragraphs

The following tips may help the readability of a document:

- break text into appropriate paragraphs of reasonable length
- if appropriate, make sub-headings within the text
- headings should be in a larger font size than body text
- leave a blank line between paragraphs
- make the margins wide enough to allow room for comments to be easily written. This can help when you revise drafts.

What are headers and footers?

For a document with many pages, information identifying the document can be included on each page. Information at the top of each page is called a header, at the bottom it is called a footer. Figure 4.12 shows the position of a header and a footer

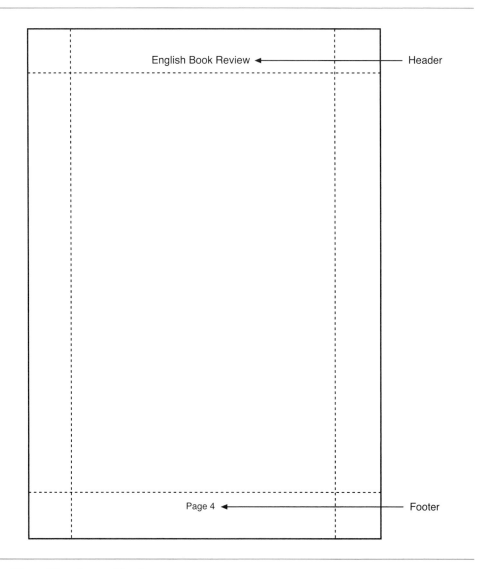

Figure 4.12   Position of header and footer

How to set out headers and footers

Figure 4.13 shows where to position a header. Where possible make the header and footer one line. The font for a header or footer can be different from the rest of the text.

Left margin · English Book Review · Automatic page number · Page 4 · Right tab setting · Right margin

Figure 4.13   The layout of a header or footer

It is usual to put the page number in a header or footer. After opening up the header or footer, key in the work 'Page' and the code or symbol to engage automatic numbering.

Your turn

1 Set up a header for an assignment that you have to hand in.
2 How would you save the details so you could adapt it to another assignment later?

Review Questions

1 List the four most important advantages of using a word processor for writing.
2 Explain what 'word wrap' means.
3 How often should a document file be saved?
4 The following steps are involved in the creation of a document. List them in their most likely order. Compare your answer with Figure 4.2 (page 38).

- ◆ enter information
- ◆ name the document/file
- ◆ edit the hard copy
- ◆ create a backup copy of the file
- ◆ edit the document on the screen
- ◆ print a hard copy of the document
- ◆ check the page set-up and alter the default settings
- ◆ run the spelling checker through the document

5 What is a cursor? List the ways a cursor can be moved around a document. How is the cursor used to insert or move text?
6 How is text in a word processor selected?
7 When would you use copy and paste rather than cut and paste?
8 Distinguish between the following: a character; a word; a sentence; a paragraph.
9 Explain the following parts of a page: top margin; left margin; right margin; left margin.
10 What should you look for when editing a document?
11 How useful are spelling checkers? In your answer give examples of errors that will and will not be detected by a spelling checker.

12 Briefly explain the ways a word processor can justify paragraphs.

13 How are the 'Times' and 'Helvetica' fonts different?

 # Tasks

Using a suitable word processing package:

1 Write an advertisement for a car boot sale your school is planning. Put the address, details of space, cost and the date and time in the advertisement.

2 Write a notice for the births column in your local newspaper.

3 Write a review of your favourite television programme. In your review list the main characters and explain why the programme appeals to you. Confine your review to 200 words.

4 Write a brief profile of your favourite pet, pop star, sports star or public figure.

5 Imagine you are planning a two week hiking holiday in Wales staying in Youth Hostels. What are the most important things you would need to carry in your back-pack? Write a brief note listing your important articles explaining why you have chosen each item.

Letters

Letters

A letter is an important method of communication. The purpose of a letter is to communicate effectively with a person or an organisation. There are commonly accepted ways for setting out a letter.

Word processing a letter

A letter is a document commonly produced by a word processor. A letter should be set out as simply as possible with the minimum of punctuation. Good setting out makes a letter easy to read. This means the letter will make a favourable impression on the reader.

Why use a word processor to write a letter?

Using a word processor to write a letter means:

- it is easier to read
- spelling checks can be made
- name and address details can be copied and pasted from other documents and applications using mail merge
- it can be prepared in advance to meet common situations
- it can be stored on disk for future reference.

A personal letter

Personal letters are written to family members, acquaintances and friends. Most personal letters do not require or ask for a reply. A personal letter may be written to:

- reply to an invitation you have received
- a friend, perhaps a penfriend
- to pass on 'news'
- congratulate a person for something they have achieved
- a newspaper or magazine in response to a current issue.

Parts of a personal letter

The mains parts of a personal letter are:

- the sender's address
- the date
- an opening greeting
- the body of letter
- the complimentary close
- signature (handwritten)
- printed name of writer (this can be omitted in some instances)

Formatting a personal letter

Figure 5.1 shows how to format a personal letter. The number of times the ENTER key is pressed after each section is shown on the right-hand side.

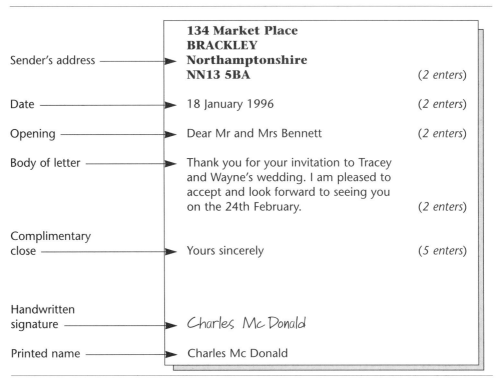

Sender's address	**134 Market Place**
	BRACKLEY
	Northamptonshire
	NN13 5BA *(2 enters)*
Date	18 January 1996 *(2 enters)*
Opening	Dear Mr and Mrs Bennett *(2 enters)*
Body of letter	Thank you for your invitation to Tracey and Wayne's wedding. I am pleased to accept and look forward to seeing you on the 24th February. *(2 enters)*
Complimentary close	Yours sincerely *(5 enters)*
Handwritten signature	*Charles Mc Donald*
Printed name	Charles Mc Donald

Figure 5.1   Example of a personal letter

Your turn

1 Do you receive letters? From whom?
2 Do you write letters? If so, to whom?
3 To whom do your parents send letters and who do they receive letters from?
4 What are the advantages of writing letters using a word processor?
5 On 24 October 1995 the National Lottery Charities Board announced the first cash grants to charities from the monies received from the National Lottery. The Board were overwhelmed with more than 15,000 applications for grants. In this first pay out about 2000, mainly small community based projects, received a total of £40 million. The Board received much criticism about which charities received the funds, but the *Daily Mirror* COMMENT 24 October expressed a different view. (See page 63).

   Do you agree with the *Daily Mirror* editorial writer? Express an opinion in a letter to the editor. State which Charities you think ought to benefit and how much Camelot should take in profits.
   The address is Daily Mirror, 1 Canada Square, London E14 5AP.

6 You have just returned home after spending two weeks holiday at your uncle's home. Write a letter to thank him for the holiday.

COMMENT

Awards must be bigger

THE people on the National Lottery Charities Board who yesterday handed out £40 million are understandably aggrieved.

In return they received a small amount of thanks, a lot of grumbles and some very nasty criticism.

Having to choose between the merits of different charities was never going to be easy. In the circumstances, the Board has done a great deal of good.

Money has gone to the disabled, the homeless and the disadvantaged. Any family that has cared for someone with a drink or drug problem knows these are as much an illness as any other.

The complaints the *Mirror* has are not over the way the Board distributed these first grants to charities.

What is wrong is that not enough of the millions brought in by the Lottery's success is going to charity.

Even worse, it seems that some of yesterday's awards made up for cuts in Government grants. That is precisely what should NOT be happening to Lottery funds.

Some of the petty moans about where the charity awards are going are pathetic. That is not the issue.

What must be looked at – and urgently – is switching more Lottery money to charities.

The Royal National Institute for the Blind was given £180,000 yesterday. But it has been losing £500,000 a year in contributions since the Lottery started.

The Government must switch some of the money which goes to the other 'good causes' to charities. And Camelot could give up some of its £1 million-a-week profits, too.

If the total handout was big enough, there would be even less reason to complain about where the money is going.

A personal business letter

A personal business letter is a formal letter to people with whom you have or would like to have a business relationship. It may be in reply to a letter they have sent to you. Letters provide a record of a communication.

A personal business letter could be written:

- to a prospective employer regarding a job application
- to a bank, insurance company or other business
- to a government body
- to your local Member of Parliament about a matter of concern.

People who hold office on bodies such as a school Governing body, charitable, social or sporting organisations often write letters. These letters may be to:

- advise members of annual meetings
- advise committee members of monthly meetings
- advise members of special activities
- businesses asked for support or donations for fund raising purposes
- a newspaper or magazine in response to a current issue.

Parts of a personal business letter

The parts of a personal business letter are:

- the sender's address (perhaps on pre-printed letterhead)
- date
- receiver's address
- opening greeting
- body of letter
- complimentary close
- signature (handwritten)
- printed name and title (if any) of the sender.

Formatting a personal business letter

Figure 5.2 shows an example of a personal business letter.

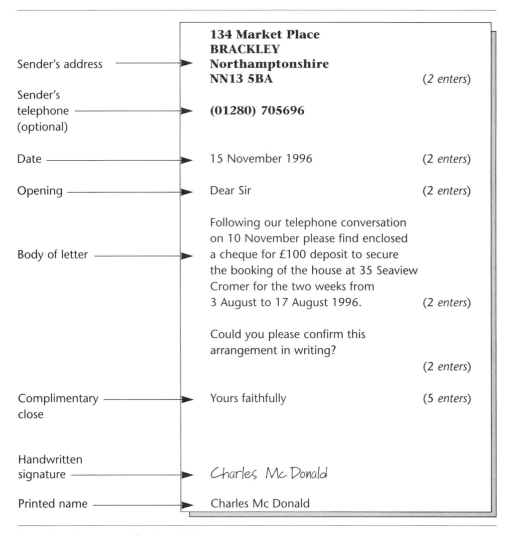

Sender's address → **134 Market Place**
BRACKLEY
Northamptonshire
NN13 5BA *(2 enters)*

Sender's telephone (optional) → **(01280) 705696**

Date → 15 November 1996 *(2 enters)*

Opening → Dear Sir *(2 enters)*

Body of letter → Following our telephone conversation on 10 November please find enclosed a cheque for £100 deposit to secure the booking of the house at 35 Seaview Cromer for the two weeks from 3 August to 17 August 1996. *(2 enters)*

Could you please confirm this arrangement in writing? *(2 enters)*

Complimentary close → Yours faithfully *(5 enters)*

Handwritten signature → *Charles McDonald*

Printed name → Charles Mc Donald

Figure 5.2   Example of a personal business letter

Your turn

1 Your local council is considering passing a law to ban completely the use of domestic bonfires. The aim is to improve the quality of air and encourage people to recycle their waste. Write a letter to your local council informing them of your views about the law and give reasons to support your view.

2 The local supermarket is advertising in the local paper for staff to work on Saturday afternoons. Write a letter expressing your interest in the position. Use the address details for a supermarket near you and address the letter to the manager.

How should an address appear in a letter?

The address in the letter should be the same as on the envelope. A standard format for use on envelopes is provided by the Royal Mail.

Figure 5.3 shows how an address should appear on a letter. Notice that you should omit punctuation in the address.

• The addressee's name	***The Secretary***
• A building number *(or name if it does not have a number)* and street name	***Post Office User's National Council***
	6 Hurcules Road
	(space)
• Locality Name *(if required - village)*	
• POST TOWN *(in block capitals)*	***LONDON***
• The County name *(if required*)*	
• POSTCODE *(in block capitals)*	***SE1 7DN***
	(space)

*(*The County name is **NOT** needed for 100 larger postal towns and 12 Scottish Isles e.g. BELFAST/SKYE and for 34 County names there are recognised abbreviations e.g. Glos for Gloucestershire)*

Figure 5.3   Example of an address

Your turn

1 Enter your address into the word processor as it should appear in a letter.
2 Enter the addresses of two friends.
3 Enter the address of your school.
4 Find and enter the address of your: local District County Council; nearest Post Office; Member of Parliament; nearest police station.
5 Send a letter to a penfriend overseas. How would the address appear in the letter?

Addressing a letter to an organisation

If a letter is to an organisation, write to the office bearer who holds the appropriate position. For example, write to the Editor of a newspaper or the Secretary of a club.

How to address a letter to a specific person

When you know the name of the person, include their title as well. For example a job advertisement would usually give details of a specific person and their title:

Ms A Girwan

Human Resource Manager

Hill & Smith Engineering Ltd

12 Oxford Road

BANBURY

Oxon

OX16 5TY

Your turn

1 Write a letter to a prominent sports personality asking him or her to speak at a school assembly about the importance of school sport.
2 Write a letter to your local Member of Parliament about a matter of concern to you; perhaps the lack of funding for I.T. education!

Other advice for letter writing

How should the date appear in a letter?

Be consistent in the use of the date form. It is generally recommended that Monday, the eleventh of March 1996 be represented by either:

◆ 11 March 1996   ◆ Monday 11 March 1996.

These forms are easy to read and require no punctuation.

How should the opening greeting appear?

For a personal letter the greeting can be informal such as 'Hello'. For a personal business letter there are a variety of greetings that are suitable. The form of the greeting depends on your relationship to the person and the formality appropriate to the letter.

Greeting	Usage
Dear Sir Dear Madam	◆ where the sex of the person is known but some formality is still required
Dear Sir/Madam	◆ if the sex of the person is unknown
Dear Mr	◆ use for man, married or unmarried
Dear Ms	◆ use for a woman, many prefer this to Mrs or Miss
Dear Mrs	◆ use for a married woman if she has indicated that this is her preferred title
Dear Miss	◆ a young girl is sometimes referred to as Miss
Dear Joanne	◆ if the letter if personal and you know the person then use a given name

Your turn

Find out the greeting that members of your family and friends prefer in letters sent to them. Does the form of the greeting depend on who is sending the letter?

How should the complimentary close appear?

For a personal letter the close to the letter can be very informal, such as 'Regards' or 'Love'. For a personal business letter the complimentary close is usually 'Yours sincerely' or 'Your faithfully'.

'Yours sincerely' is normally used if a name has been used in the opening greeting – for example, Dear Mr Allen.

'Yours faithfully' is normally used if a name has not been used in the opening greeting – for example, Dear Sir/Madam.

Where should a handwritten signature appear?

For personal and personal business letters a handwritten signature should appear between the complimentary close and the printed signature.

Page layout

Most letters are left justified. Each line begins at the left margin. Addresses on envelopes are also left justified. Figure 5.3 shows a left justified address. A handwritten signature would start close to the left margin.

Before printing a letter check that the letter is centred on the page, both vertically and horizontally.

Your turn

1 Where should the postcode for a handwritten envelope be placed?
2 Collect four examples of envelopes that arrive in your household. Do the addresses meet the requirements of the Royal Mail?

3 What forms of greeting are used on letters sent to your family?

4 Where should the postcode for a machine addressed envelope be placed?

Tips for writing and formatting letters

When word processing a letter:

- check that a person's title is correct
- check that the spelling of a person's name is correct

When addressing an envelope:

- do not underline in the address
- put a return address on the envelope

- check the postcode for an address
- start every line on the left margin.

- the address lines should be left justified.

Your turn

Find the 'Letters to the Editor' section in a newspaper. Select a letter that someone has written on a topic that you are interested in and compose a reply to that letter. What specific address details would you put on the envelope?

Review questions

1 Why might you write a personal letter?

2 In what situations would a business letter be used?

3 List the main parts of a personal letter.

4 How does a business letter differ from a personal letter in format?

5 When would you use the complimentary closes 'Yours sincerely' and 'Yours faithfully' in a letter?

6 What does 'open punctuation' mean?

7 How should an address appear in a letter?

Tasks

1 Investigate envelope sizes. What conditions must be met for a letter to be a 'standard letter' at the standard postage rate?

2 What is the postcode of the Post Office in the County town of your County?

3 How is a PO box number included in an address?

4 Find the postcodes for Stratford in the Post Codes directory in your local library. How many Stratfords did you find?

5 Find some examples of unusual addresses.

6 Graphics

What is a graphic image?

Computer graphic images are lines, curves and shapes that can be created, saved, altered, displayed and printed. The type of image generated, displayed and used depends on the:

- software used to create the image
- quality of the monitor on which the image is displayed
- type of printer used to print the image
- type of computer used to create and display the image.

How are images created?

Images are created using computer software that is operated by the keyboard and a computer mouse. It is possible to draw lines, circles, squares, rectangles, curves, freehand lines and to use a range of patterns and colours. Text may be entered using the keyboard.

Images may be created using a scanner, a drawing tablet or by tracing another drawing.

What are the features of graphics programs?

All graphics programs have the following features:

- a drawing or painting window in which the image will be created
- a palette of tools for creating the image
- the ability to move, copy and resize parts of the image.

What is a bit-mapped image?

A computer monitor is made up of a large number of picture elements or dots that are called pixels. Each pixel can be controlled by the computer and can be black or white or a colour if the computer includes a colour monitor.

Paint programs are used to tell the computer how to display each pixel. The images they create are called bit-mapped images.

Figure 6.1(a) shows an image used in Windows Paint. Figure 6.1(b) is an enlargement of the same image. Each of the pixel squares can be easily seen. The image could be modified by clicking on each square and changing it to either black or white.

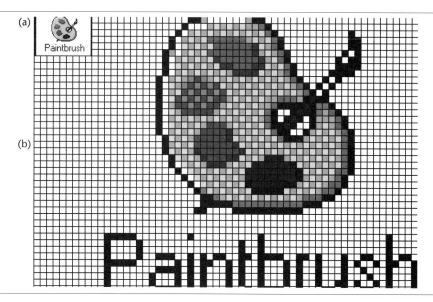

Figure 6.1   (a) Paintbrush Icon (b) Image enlarged

What is the difference between a paint program and a draw program?

Paint programs create bit-mapped images by changing individual pixels. Shapes are created and changed by using the palette of tools to access any pixel or group of pixels. Paint programs are very flexible and images can be altered very easily. Most paint programs will include an eraser tool which allows you to 'rub out' pixels.

When paint images are printed, the quality of the image depends directly on the way it has been saved. Often paint images are saved at 72 dots per inch which means that they may have jagged edges when they are printed. This is very noticeable when images are resized.

Draw programs use a mathematical formula to generate each image. Each shape that is created is an object in its own right. Each object may be moved around the window and its size or shape altered. Using a drawing program is like drawing on a number of layers of glass. Each image is on a new layer and may be moved forward or backwards.

Draw programs are generally not as flexible as paint programs but produce better quality output when printed. They are used when greater accuracy or working to a scale is required.

How is a paint program used?

A paint program is made up of a painting window, a palette of painting tools and a menu of commands that can be used. Figure 6.2 shows a typical paint program screen with the tools down the left-hand side and a window in which the image can be created and modified.

Painting tools

All paint programs require a mouse to be used to create the image. For example, Microsoft Windows Paintbrush has 18 tools and also includes a colour palette.

Figure 6.2   Typical paint screen

Each painting tool has a specific function. All paint programs will have tools that carry out these functions, although the way they operate will differ slightly. Table 6.1 (on page 72) gives an explanation of the paint tools used in Windows Paint.

 Your turn

1 Start a paint program on your computer at school. Write down the names of each of the tools that you can use to create images. Also write down a brief summary of what each tool will do.
2 Use a paint program to draw: a logo for a computer company, use geometric forms as the basis for the logo.
3 Use 'zoom' to improve detail.
4 What do you use to copy and paste part of your drawing using your paint program? Copy and paste your logo a number of times.

Table 6.1   An explanation of tools used in WINDOWS PAINT

Tool	Use		Example
			Selection tool, used to select part of the image for copying and cutting.
	Spray tool used to spray paint images.		Text tool, used to enter text into the drawing area.
	Selective eraser, only erases the foreground colour.		Eraser tool, used to erase parts of the painting.
	Fill tool, used to fill shapes or screen areas with colour.		Paint tool, used to paint lines of different weight, shape and pattern.
	Rubber band tool used to draw curved lines between two points.		Line tool, used to draw straight lines.
	Rectangle tool, used to draw rectangular and square frames with sharp corners.		Rectangle tool used to draw filled rectangles and squares.
	Rectangle tool, used to draw rectangle and square frames with rounded corners.		Rounded rectangle tool for filled rectangles with rounded corners.
	Circle tool, used to draw circular or oval lines.		Circle tool, used to draw filled ovals and circles.
	Polygon tool, used to draw straight sided shapes.		Polygon tool, used to draw filled straight sided shapes.

Colours and fills in a paint program

Paint programs will also include a palette of colours and different types of fill. See Figure 6.3. Fills are used to fill up the inside of the shape with a chosen pattern and colour.

Figure 6.3 A range of patterns used for filling a shape

A range of line sizes are also usually available. This means that lines can be drawn to any of the available thicknesses.

Example – Creating a picture of a house

This example uses a paint program to create a picture of a house. Figure 6.4 shows the completed house.

Figure 6.4 A house created using a paint program

The steps to draw the house are as follows:
1 Use the rectangle tool to draw a rectangle, fill it with a brick pattern.
2 Draw the door and window with the rectangle tool using appropriate fill colours or patterns.
3 Use the straight line tool to make the roof line.
4 Fill the roof with a pattern using the paint can tool.
5 Use the straight line tool to create a chimney and then fill it using the paint can tool.
6 Create a front path using a freehand tool or an arc tool.
7 Create a picket fence. Draw one picket using the straight line tool with a heavy weight. Use the selection tool to copy it, then paste the copy.
8 Use zoom to put details into the door and window, e.g. letterbox, handles, etc.
9 Use the select tool to copy and resize the house to show another in the background.

Your turn

1 Use a paint program to develop your painting skills on the computer. Try each of the tools in the palette. Make sure you can do the following:

   ◆ draw straight lines, using different line widths
   ◆ draw rectangles and squares, using different line widths for the sides
   ◆ erase parts of the image using the erase tool
   ◆ use zoom to improve detail
   ◆ resize drawings using the select tool with shrink and grow
   ◆ copy parts of the diagram and paste them in another part of the window.

2 Use a paint program to produce a picture of:

   ◆ a flower in a vase   ◆ a face.

3 Use a paint program to create the following:

   ◆ a picture of the front of your house with the address written underneath
   ◆ a picture of yourself.

Draw programs

Draw programs allow you to create objects rather than bit-mapped images. The objects may be moved around the screen and can be placed in front of or behind other objects.

A draw program will also have a palette of tools to be used for creating an image. Many of the draw tools in Clarisworks are similar to the paint tools. These tools are shown in Table 6.2.

Table 6.2 Draw tools used in Clarisworks. Note the similarity to paint tools

Selection arrow, used to select, move and resize objects.

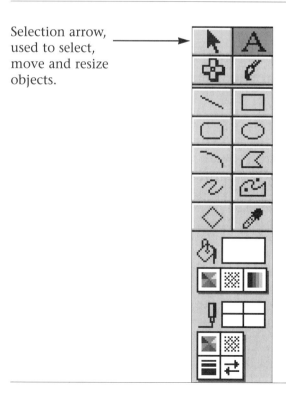

Colours and fills with a draw program

Draw programs also include a palette of colours and different types of fill. Fills are used to fill the inside of a shape with a chosen pattern and colour. Patterns and colours for the fills may often be changed within the program.

Your turn

1 Start a draw program on your computer at school. Write down the names of each of the tools that you can create images. Also write down a brief summary of what each will do.
2 Use a draw program to draw: a straight line; a rectangle and a square; a circle and an oval; a rectangle with rounded edges; a freehand line.
3 Use a draw program to create rectangles, ovals, squares and circles with different fills.

Selecting an object

The selection tool is used to select object so that they can be moved, copied, deleted, resized or rotated – see Table 6.2.

The purpose of the 'handles' are to allow an object to be moved, resized or stretched. Figure 6.5 shows an object that has been copied and then resized and stretched.

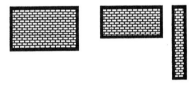

Figure 6.5   Resizing and stretching an object

Objects can also be rotated. Figure 6.6 shows an object that has been rotated through 90°.

Figure 6.6   Rotating an object

Because draw programs work in layers, objects can be moved backwards and forwards as shown in Figure 6.7.

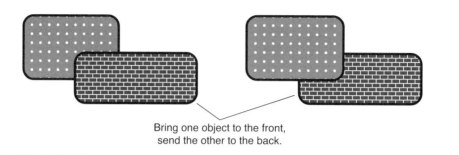

Bring one object to the front, send the other to the back.

Figure 6.7 Moving objects backwards and forwards

Objects can also be moved around in relation to one another.

Example – Creating a logo

The logo shown in Figure 6.8 was created in a draw program by carrying out the steps listed below.

Figure 6.8 Logo created using Clarisworks

1 Draw a black rectangle.
2 Draw another rectangle in front of the black rectangle, ensuring it is opaque and filled with the same shading as the background – for example, white. This gives a shadow effect.
3 Use the text tool with a large font and bold style to enter the initials 'GGB'.
4 Use a smaller font to enter the word 'Enterprises' on the next line.
5 Choose a graphics font such as Wingdings and enter a character to the left of the text.

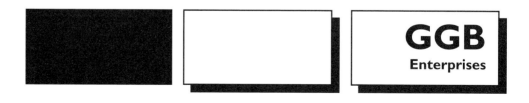

Figure 6.9 The first three steps in creating the logo

Your turn

1 Use a draw program to make sure you can do the following:

- ◆ draw straight lines of varying thicknesses
- ◆ select an object, copy and paste it a number of times
- ◆ use the text tool to key in a sentence, select the text and try different fonts, sizes and styles

- ◆ draw squares, both empty and filled with a pattern
- ◆ draw circles, both filled with a pattern and empty
- ◆ draw overlapping objects, select one and move it backwards and forwards.

2 Follow the steps in the example above to create a logo with your initials.
3 Collect a file of logos from advertisements, leaflets, and business cards. Identify from the collection what makes a successful logo.
4 Design a logo for your family.
5 Create a map of your street showing the location of your house.

Clip art

Clip art refers to a range of images that are supplied on disk and may be copied onto your own program. There is a large range of clip art topics available, from sport to education to people. Many of these are available as shareware or public domain programs.

The images are copied by selecting them with a selection tool and then using the copy command before pasting them into a document or program.

Figure 6.10   Example of clip from ClarisImpact

What is a 'scanner'?

A scanner is a device which copies an image and creates and stores it on a computer disk in a form that can be used by a computer. A scanner is a piece of hardware that is connected to a computer by a cable, plus software that allows the computer to interpret the image from the scanner.

A scanner works rather like a photocopies. The original is placed on a glass plate, the lid is put down and a button is pressed. A light comes on as the image is scanned and the result is sent to the computer to be stored on disk.

The image can be edited on the computer using the software that comes with the scanner or saved and altered using other graphics software. The image, or parts of it, can then be copied and used in other applications.

A scanner can be used to produce either paint or draw images and with character recognition software can scan and import text to a word processor. The type of image that is produced depends on the image that is scanned and the use to which the image will be put.

Figure 6 11   A scanned photograph

If a scanned photograph is to be printed out, it will need to be saved as a paint type image. Photographs usually need to be scanned in this way because they include a range of greys that are best represented by each different pixel. Figure 6.11 shows an example of a photograph that has been scanned and then printed out.

If the original is only black and white, it is called line art. It can be scanned as line art and the image can be saved in a draw format. The image can then be copied into a graphics program and resized and edited. This is particularly useful for diagrams and sketches. Scanning a logo as line art is an example of such a use.

How is an image scanned?

The steps in scanning are:
- place the image in the scanner
- run the scanning software
- preview the graphic on the computer monitor
- select the part of the image to be scanned
- scan the image
- edit the image – perhaps crop or touch it up using the tools provided with the scanning software
- save the image.

 Your turn

1 Use a scanner to scan a piece of line art, save it and print it out. How much space does the file take up on the disk?
2 Use a scanner to scan a photograph of yourself. Save the image and then print it out. How much space does the file take up on disk?

Review questions

1 List the main differences between paint and draw programs.

2 Using either a paint or a draw program, answer the following questions.
   a Which tools do you use to draw polygons?
   b How do you work on individual pixels to improve definition?
   c How do you change or add to the colour/pattern palette?
   d How do you copy and resize parts of an image?

3 What is clip art? How can it be used in a graphics program?

4 What is a scanner?
  What steps would you take to scan part of a photograph?

 # Tasks

1 Create your own business card. A business card is usually about 9.5cm in width and 5.5cm in length. You will need to copy your logo and put it on the card. Business cards usually include the employee's name, title, company name, address and telephone number.

2 Create your own letterhead using your logo and including your name and address.

3 Draw a plan of your home.

4 Design a cover for a compact disc to be recorded by your favourite singer or group. Compact disc covers are usually about 12.5cm by 14.0cm in size.

5 Copy an item of clip art into a paint program and modify the image.

6 Scan a photograph of your favourite pop group and use it in a promotion leaflet for a forthcoming concert.

7 Scan a logo from a newspaper or magazine. Edit the image to make sure it is complete. Save the logo and use it in creating a business card.

8 Use a flat bed scanner and a hand-held scanner to scan part of a photograph. What are the differences in using each of these types of scanner? Are the results any different?

9 Use clip art in the design of a notice to promote a Tutor group outing to an ice rink.

Spreadsheets

7

What is a spreadsheet?

A spreadsheet is a large sheet of paper onto which numbers and text are entered in rows and columns. Where each row and column meet is called a cell. Each cell contains numbers or text.

Almost any type of calculation that can be set up in rows and columns can be done with a spreadsheet. A spreadsheet is made up of many individual cells. Your school will probably use a version of EXCEL, check how many cells it contains.

Figure 7.1 shows a typical use of a spreadsheet. The calculation takes up 7 rows, 6 columns (42 cells) of the spreadsheet. It contains information about sales over a twelve month period.

Rows are usually numbered from 1 to 16 382 or however many rows there are in the spreadsheet. Columns are usually identified by letters from A to Z then AA, AB...AZ, BA, BB...BZ and so on.

Each cell can contain a:

◆ number – for example, 45, 66.55, –8889
◆ piece of text – for example, John Smith, July
◆ formula – for example, =A1*2 which multiplies the value in cell A1 by 2

◆ function – for example, =sum(A1:A12) which adds up the values of all the cells from A1 to A12.

In Figure 7.1, the cells contain numbers, text and formulae. Using a formula allows complex calculations to be carried out very quickly.

Why use a spreadsheet?

A spreadsheet is a very good way to solve problems that use a lot of calculations. Some examples of typical uses for a spreadsheet are:

◆ arranging information in a table
◆ finding out how much interest can be earned over a period of time with a particular investment

◆ preparing a budget
◆ working out how much money must be repaid when taking out a loan.

How is a spreadsheet organised?

The location of a cell is referred to by the column then the row, for example cell B5, refers to column B, row 5.

The active cell refers to the cell that is being worked on at that instant

The contents of the active cell appear in the formula bar. The names along the top are the various menus that include the commands that can be used with the spreadsheet. Figure 7.1 shows some of the main parts of a spreadsheet.

	A	B	C	D	E	F
1		Gina's Profit Report 1995				
2						
3		Summer	Autumn	Winter	Spring	Total
4						
5	Revenue	£12,345	£13,580	£12,901	£13,546	£52,372
6	Costs	£8,944	£10,286	£9,874	£10,565	£39,669
7	Profit	£3,401	£3,294	£3,027	£2,981	£12,703

Figure 7.1 The main parts of a spreadsheet

Your turn

1 Write down what is contained in the following cells in Figure 7.1: A5, E7, F3.
2 Looking at Figure 7.1, write down the cell references for: Summer, £3401, Gina's Profit Report 1995.

Moving around a spreadsheet

The screen can display only a part of the spreadsheet at any one time. This display is called a window. Any part of the spreadsheet may be displayed in a window by moving the cursor. The cursor may be moved by using:

- the arrow keys
- a mouse
- the TAB key

- the scroll bars
- PAGE UP or PAGE DOWN keys
- the GO TO function.

Your turn

1 Read the manual for the spreadsheet which you use. Write down all the ways that the cursor can be moved around the screen.
2 Start the spreadsheet program and use each of these ways to move the cursor around the screen. Move to the last row, then to the last column. What is the cell reference of the cell in the last row and last column?
3 Move the cursor to the cell with the reference G110 and write down what you did to get there.

How is text entered?

Text can be entered in a cell by making that cell active and using the keyboard to type in the text. Once the text is correct, use the ENTER key to accept it.

Text is used to provide meaning to the spreadsheet by providing headings and labels for cells, rows and columns. Labels help explain what the numbers in a cell represent.

Example – Going to the cinema

This example uses a spreadsheet to work out the cost of going to the cinema. The costs might include transport, the cost of the ticket, refreshments at interval, and a soft drink after the show.

First set up the text headings:

- create a heading in the first row of the second column, cell B1
- in the first column, starting at A3, enter labels for each row: transport, ticket, food, drink
- in A8, enter the label 'TOTAL'.

The spreadsheet is shown in Figure 7.2.

	A	B	C	D
1		Cost of Going to the Cinema		
2				
3	Transport			
4	Ticket			
5	Food			
6	Drink			
7				
8	TOTAL			

Figure 7.2   Going to the cinema spreadsheet

The width of a column may need to be changed to ensure that all of the text can be displayed. One method is to choose the column width command and enter the appropriate value.

Your turn

1 Use a spreadsheet to enter the text in the 'Going to the cinema' example and save the spreadsheet calling it 'cinema'.
2 Use a spreadsheet to enter your school timetable. It should look something like Figure 7.3. Print the spreadsheet when it is complete.
3 For each of the following, create the row and column headings that would be needed for the problem.
   a Create headings in a spreadsheet to work out the cost of buying a new car. Costs will include purchase price, car tax, number plates, delivery, road fund licence, insurance and any extra items such as in car entertainment, air bags, etc...
   b Create headings in a spreadsheet that compares the prices of four different cars. Use advertisements in the newspaper to find the names and models of the cars. Use a column headed 'Price' with a row for each type of car you identify.
   c Create headings in a spreadsheet that will keep track of your marks in your school subjects. You will need to enter a suitable heading and the names of all the subjects you are studying.

	A	B	C	D	E	F
1		**Matthew's Year 8 School Timetable**				
2		**Monday**	**Tuesday**	**Wednesday**	**Thursday**	**Friday**
3	1	Science	Humanities	Music	P.E.	Mathematics
4	2	Science	French	Drama	Mathematics	Science
5	Break					
6	3	Technology	Mathematics	Humanities	English	Art
7	4	Humanities	English	Humanities	I.T.	Art
8	Lunch					
9	5	P.E.	Technology	English	Science	French
10	6	P.E.	Technology	French	Science	Mathematics

Figure 7.3   A school timetable

How are numbers entered?

Numbers can be entered in a cell by making that cell active using the mouse to point and click and then using the keyboard to type in the number. Press the ENTER key once the number has been entered.

A wide range of operations can be carried out using numbers including addition, subtraction, multiplication and division.

Example – Going to the cinema

The costs of transport (£1.80), ticket (£3.75), food (£2.99), and a drink (£.90) give the following spreadsheet (figure 7.4).

	A	B	C	D
1		Cost of Going to the Cinema		
2				
3	Transport	1.8		
4	Ticket	3.75		
5	Food	2.75		
6	Drink	0.9		
7				
8	TOTAL			

Figure 7.4   Going to the cinema spreadsheet

Note that the width of column A has been altered to show all the text.

Your turn

1 Enter the numbers in the 'Going to the cinema' example into your 'CINEMA' spreadsheet.
2 For each of Questions 3a to c in the Your turn on the previous page, enter the costs and amounts of money you have found in the appropriate cells.

How are numbers formatted?

Numbers are displayed by the spreadsheet in a variety of ways. The number 765 could be entered, selected and formatted as:

◆ integers (whole numbers)   765
◆ a number of decimal places   765.00
◆ money   £765 or £765.00
◆ a percentage   76.5%

Each spreadsheet package includes a number of different ways of displaying the same number. Numbers can also be used to represent days and time, for example, 140593 can be used for the date 14 May 1993.

In Figure 7.4 above, the numbers have not been formatted in any way. Selecting the cells B3 to B6 and formatting them as money gives the cells shown in Figure 7.5.

	A	B	C	D
1		Cost of Going to the Cinema		
2				
3	Transport	£1.80		
4	Ticket	£3.75		
5	Food	£2.75		
6	Drink	£0.90		
7				
8	TOTAL			

Figure 7.5   Going to the cinema spreadsheet

Your turn

1 Look at the spreadsheet you are using and write down how many different ways it allows you to format numbers.
2 Go back to the spreadsheets created above and format the numbers so that all money amounts have £ signs in front of them. Large numbers should be formatted as whole numbers and small amounts as pounds and pence.

What is a formula?

A formula is used for making calculations. It usually consists of an '=' sign, one or more cell references and operators such as '+' for addition or '−' for subtraction. Note that in some spreadsheets, a formula starts with a '+' sign.

The formula '=A5+1' means take the value of cells A5, add 1 to it and place the result in the active cell. Figure 7.6 shows the value 45 in cell A5, the formula '=A5+1' in cell A6 which has the value of 46.

	A
1	
2	
3	
4	
5	45
6	46
7	
8	

	A
1	
2	
3	
4	
5	45
6	=A5+1
7	
8	

Figure 7.6   Using a formula in a spreadsheet

In calculating the cost of going to the cinema, cell B8 will need a formula to work out the total cost. The results are shown in Figure 7.7.

(a)

	A	B
1		Cost of Going to the Cinema
2		
3	Transport	£1.80
4	Ticket	£3.75
5	Food	£2.75
6	Drink	£0.90
7		
8	TOTAL	£9.20

(b)

	A	B
1		Cost of Going to the Cinema
2		
3	Transport	1.8
4	Ticket	3.75
5	Food	2.75
6	Drink	0.9
7		
8	TOTAL	=B6+B5+B4+B3

Figure 7.7   The cost of going to the cinema

Cell B8 contains the formula '=B6+B5+B4+B3'. The formula may be entered by typing in an equals sign followed by the cell references in the formula box. Another method is to enter the equals sign and then click on each of the cells to be added together. The formula is shown in Figure 7.7(b).

Your turn

1 How is a formula entered in the spreadsheet you use? How can it be altered?
2 Key in the spreadsheet in Figure 7.8 and save it as '**HOUSE**' – note B2 = 1% of B1.
3 Modify the spreadsheets you have created in the Your turn on page 83 to include simple formulae for the totals where appropriate.

	A	B
1	Purchase Price	£80,000
2	Stamp duty	£800
3	Solicitor's fee	£300
4	Valuation fee	£250
5	Removal firm	£750
6	TOTAL	£82,100

Figure 7.8   Spreadsheet showing the cost of buying a house

Using a function

Another way of doing additions is to use a function. A function in EXCEL is made up of:

- an '=' sign
- a function name
- brackets or parentheses
- an argument – usually a range of cells to be used in the calculation.

Thus, B6 in Figure 7.8 could contain the function '=SUM(B1:B5)'.

In this case the function name is 'SUM' and the argument or range refers to all the cells from B1 to B5 inclusive.

Every spreadsheet has a range of functions. Another useful function is 'AVERAGE' which calculates the average of the numbers in the specified range. For example, Figure 7.9 shows the runs scored for six cricketers with the average calculated in column F.

	A	B	C	D	E	F
1	Name	Scores				Average
2						
3	Dhaliwal	25	56	45	2	32.00
4	Hussain	0	12	141	45	49.50
5	Smith	12	45	22	31	27.50
6	Bennett	45	87	56	3	47.75
7	Peters	25	54	65	71	53.75
8	Khan	12	8	111	65	49.00

Figure 7.9   Spreadsheet showing average runs scored

Figure 7.10 shows the same spreadsheet with the function for the average in column F.

	A	B	C	D	E	F
1	Name	Scores				Average
2						
3	Dhaliwal	25	56	45	2	=AVERAGE(B3:E3)
4	Hussain	0	12	141	45	=AVERAGE(B4:E4)
5	Smith	12	45	22	31	=AVERAGE(B5:E5)
6	Bennett	45	87	56	3	=AVERAGE(B6:E6)
7	Peters	25	54	65	71	=AVERAGE(B7:E7)
8	Khan	12	8	111	65	=AVERAGE(B8:E8)

Figure 7.10   Spreadsheet showing the function in column F.

Your turn

1 How is a function entered in the spreadsheet you use? How can it be altered?
2 Modify the spreadsheet you saved as 'HOUSE' to use the 'SUM' function to work out the total cost.
3 Modify the spreadsheet you have created in the Your turn on page 83 to include a function for the totals where appropriate.
4 Use a spreadsheet to enter the goals scored by each Premier League Football team last weekend (or use the results from another sport which interests you) and use the AVERAGE function to calculate the average goals scored.

What happens if the value in a cell is changed?

What happens to the cost of going to the cinema if the price of the ticket goes up but you spend less on food and drink? Figure 7.11 shows the results.

	A	B	C
1		Cost of Going to the Cinema	
2			
3	Transport	£1.80	
4	Ticket	£4.00	
5	Food	£2.50	
6	Drink	£0.95	
7			
8	TOTAL	£9.25	

Figure 7.11   Going to the cinema after prices have changed

The new total cost is calculated and displayed in cell B8.

Example – Buying a house

What happens if the purchase price of the house is changed? Entering a new value in that cell immediately results in a new value in cell B8 (and B4). See Figure 7.12.

	A	B
1	Purchase price	£85,000
2	Stamp duty	£850
3	Solicitor's fee	£300
4	Valuation fee	£250
5	Removal firm	£750
6	TOTAL	£87,150

Figure 7.12   Changing the cost of buying a house

Your turn

1   Enter the new amounts in your spreadsheet called 'HOUSE' and check the value of the total.
2   Alter the figures in your spreadsheets from the Your turn on page 83 and note what happens to the results.

Copying cells

Text, numbers and formulae can be copied from one cell to another, just like using a word processor.

Example – Buying a house

What happens if you wish to compare the cost of two different houses? Create a second column by adding the new numbers plus a heading in cell C1. However, the total cell can be created by copying it from B7. Select B7, copy it, move to cell C7 and paste it. The spreadsheet in Figure 7.13 is the result.

	A	B	C
1		House 1	House 2
2	Purchase price	£85,000	£90,000
3	Stamp duty	£850	£900
4	Solicitor's fee	£300	£300
5	Valuation fee	£250	£250
6	Removal firm	£750	£750
7	TOTAL	£87,150	£92,200

Figure 7.13   Comparing the cost of two houses

The formula is copied from cell B7 to cell C7 and is shown in Figure 7.14.

	A	B	C
7	TOTAL	= SUM(B2:B6)	= SUM(C2:C6)

Figure 7.14   Copied formulae

Example – Comparing the cinema and football

Compare the cost of going to the cinema with the cost of going to a football match (home match where you are a member).
   Select cell B2 to B7, copy them and paste them into cells C2 to C7.

Now, alter the text in cell C1 and the numbers in cells C2 to C5. The new result appears in cell C7, as shown in Figure 7.15.

	A	B	C
1		cinema	football
2	Transport	£1.80	£2.50
3	Ticket	£4.00	£8.00
4	Food	£2.50	£2.75
5	Drink	£0.95	£0.65
6			
7	TOTAL	£9.25	£13.90

Figure 7.15 Comparing costs

The formula is also copied from cell B7 to cell C7, as shown in Figure 7.16.

	A	B	C
7	TOTAL	= B5 + B4 + B3 + B2	= C5 + C4 + C3 + C2

Figure 7.16 Copied formulae

Your turn

1 Alter your 'cinema' spreadsheet to compare the cost of going to the cinema and going to a football match.
2 Alter your 'HOUSE' spreadsheet to compare the cost of two different houses.
3 Alter your spreadsheet which compares the cost of different cars to add a column that has the cost of last year's model.

What is a relative reference?

The formula for calculating the total cost of going to the cinema in cell B8 is '=B6+B5+B4+B3'.

Stored in B8 is a formula which says: 'Add the value of the cell two cells up and the value of the cell three cells up and the value of the cell four cells up and the value of the cell five cells up.' Thus, when it is copied to cell C8 it works correctly, adding up the numbers in column C.

These are called relative cell references because they refer to cells by their position compared to the active cell. Figure 7.17 shows relative references.

	A	B
1		Cost of Going to the Cinema
2		
3	Transport	1.8
4	Ticket	3.75
5	Food	2.75
6	Drink	0.9
7		
8	TOTAL	= B6 + B5 + B4 + B3

Figure 7.17 Relative references

Using Fill Down and Fill Right

The Fill Down and Fill Right commands are used to copy the contents of a cell into a range of adjacent cells.

The Fill Down command can, for example, be used to create a series of numbers from 1 to 10. The number 1 is entered into cell A1 and the formula '=A1+1' in cell A2. See Figure 7.18.

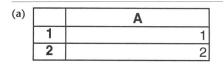
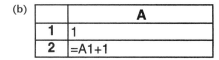

(a)

	A
1	1
2	2

(b)

	A
1	1
2	=A1+1

Figure 7.18   (a) Screen display (b) Entering the formula

Now cells A2 through A12 are selected and the Fill Down command is used. The screen display that results and the actual cell contents are shown in Figure 7.19.

(a)

	A
1	1
2	2
3	3
4	4
5	5
6	6
7	7
8	8
9	9
10	10
11	11
12	12

(b)

	A
1	1
2	=A1+1
3	=A2+1
4	=A3+1
5	=A4+1
6	=A5+1
7	=A6+1
8	=A7+1
9	=A8+1
10	=A9+1
11	=A10+1
12	=A11+1

Figure 7.19   (a) Screen display (b) Actual cell references

The relative reference is copied from cell A2 into cells A3, A4...A12, with the numbers 2 through 12 being the result of the calculation. Remember that '=A1+1' means 'add 1 to the cell above' as do '=A2+1',... '=A11+1'.

Using the Fill Right command, a similar operation can be carried out to create a row of relative references, as shown in Figure 7.20(b). This results in the numbers from 1 to 6 being displayed in the spreadsheet, as shown in Figure 7.20(a).

(a)

	A	B	C	D	E	F
1	1	2	3	4	5	6
2	2	4	6	8	10	12

(b)

	A	B	C	D	E	F
1	1	=A1+1	=B1+1	=C1+1	=D1+1	=E1+1
2	=A1+1	=A2+2	=B2+2	=C2+2	=D2+2	=E2+2

Figure 7.20   (a) The results using the Fill Right command   (b) Creating a row of relative references

The process of using the Fill Down and Fill Right commands to create new cells is called 'replication'.

Your turn

1 Use the Fill Down command to enter the numbers from 1 to 20 in column A starting at cell A1.
2 Use the Fill Right command to enter the numbers from 1 to 12 in row 1 starting at cell A1.
3 Enter the number 2 in cell A1 of a spreadsheet, then the formula '=A1*2' in cell A2. Select cells A2 through to A10 and fill down. What numbers appear in cells A3 to A10? What is the formula in each of those cells?

Example – Creating a multiplication table

The Fill Down command can be used to create a multiplication table for any given number. This process is described below.

- Enter the heading 'Number' in cell A1 and the number 5 in cell A3.
- Enter the formula '=A3' in cell A4.
- Select cells A4 to A14 and choose Fill Down. This will put the number 5 in a column of twelve cells.
- Enter the symbol for multiplication (*) in cell B3 and then select cells B3 to B14 and choose Fill Down. This puts the * sign in each cell.

- Use a similar method to put an '=' sign in cells D3 to D14.
- Enter the number 1 in cell C3, the formula '=C3+1' in cell C4 and then select C4 to C14 and choose Fill Down. This puts the numbers 1 to 12 in cells C3 to C14.
- In cell E3 enter the formula '=A3*C3', then select cells C3 to C14 and choose Fill Down. The result and cell contents are shown in Figure 7.21

	A	B	C	D	E
1	Number				Result
2					
3	5	*	1	=	5
4	5	*	2	=	10
5	5	*	3	=	15
6	5	*	4	=	20
7	5	*	5	=	25
8	5	*	6	=	30
9	5	*	7	=	35
10	5	*	8	=	40
11	5	*	9	=	45
12	5	*	10	=	50
13	5	*	11	=	55
14	5	*	12	=	60

Figure 7.21   Screen display and actual cell references

Entering a new number in cell A3 creates a new multiplication table.

Your turn
Create the multiplication table in the previous example following the steps given. What happens if the number in cell A3 is changed from 5 to 6?

What is an absolute reference?

When you want to store a reference to a cell that will not change with the copy or fill command, you must refer to the absolute cell reference. In many spreadsheets, this is done by using $ signs in the cell reference.

Example – Increasing the price

A trader decides to increase the price of each item of stock by 10 per cent. Five items of stock are affected by this price increase. The value 10 per cent is entered in cell B1. This will be used to work out the increase in the price of each item. Item A has a price of £50.00 (cell B4). The price increase is calculated by multiplying the value in cell B4 by the value in cell B1. The result, £5.00, is stored in cell C4. To get the new price add cells B4 and C4 and store the result in cell D4. See Figure 7.22.

The formula that is entered in cell C4 is '=B4*B1'. This formula means that to get the price increase in cell C4, you multiply the contents of cells B4 and B1. The formula for cell D4 is '=B4+C4'.

	A	B	C	D
1	Percentage	10%		
2				
3	Stock Item	Old Price	Increase	New Price
4	Item A	£50.00	£5.00	£55.00
5	Item B	£123.00	£12.30	£135.30
6	Item C	£28.00	£2.80	£30.80
7	Item D	£45.55	£4.56	£50.11
8	Item E	£258.00	£25.80	£283.80

Figure 7.22   Calculating a price increase

This process is repeated for each item. For item B, multiply the values in cells B5 and B1 and store the result in C5. Then add cells B5 and C5 and store the result in cell D5.

The $ sign shows that when the formula is created by copying to the cells below it always refers to the cell B1. That is, B1 is an absolute reference. This is shown in Figure 7.23.

	A	B	C	D
1	Percentage	0.1		
2				
3	Stock Item	Old Price	Increase	New Price
4	Item A	50	=B4*B1	=B4+C4
5	Item B	123	=B5*B1	=B5+C5
6	Item C	28	=B6*B1	=B6+C6
7	Item D	45.55	=B7*B1	=B7+C7
8	Item E	258	=B8*B1	=B8+C8

Figure 7.23   Actual cell references

'What if' analysis

When important data on a spreadsheet is changed, a new result is immediately calculated. This is called 'What if' analysis. For example, what if the rate of increase in the product price was 15 per cent instead of 10 per cent? Entering 15 per cent in cell B1 causes the spreadsheet to recalculate the results.

'What if' analysis is used to check what happens when figures change. It is particularly useful when working out figures that involve money.

Your turn

1 Enter the spreadsheet in Figure 7.22, making sure that cell B1 contains an absolute reference. Change the value in cell B1 to 15 per cent, 20 per cent and 5 per cent and write down the new prices in each case.

2 Enter the spreadsheet in Figure 7.24 below which calculates the value of a house over time. Assume that the purchase price is £80,000 and that the house will increase in value at the rate of 5 per cent each year. Note that the formulae in column B refer to an absolute reference for cell B2. Change the values of B1 and B2 to answer the following questions.

a What would the value of the house be after 10 years if the annual inflation rate is 10%?

b What would the value of the house be after 10 years if prices fell by an average of 2% per year?

c What would the value of a house that cost £125,000 be after 10 years if the annual inflation rate was 1, 2 or 5 per cent?

(a)

	A	B
1	House value	£80,000
2	Inflation rate	5%
3		
4	Year	House Value
5		
6	0	£80,000
7	1	£84,000
8	2	£88,200
9	3	£92,610
10	4	£97,241
11	5	£102,103
12	6	£107,208
13	7	£112,568
14	8	£118,196
15	9	£124,106
16	10	£130,312

(b)

	A	B
1	House value	80000
2	Inflation rate	0.05
3		
4	Year	House Value
5		
6	0	= B1
7	1	= B6*(1 + B2)
8	2	= B7*(1 + B2)
9	3	= B8*(1 + B2)
10	4	= B9*(1 + B2)
11	5	= B10*(1 + B2)
12	6	= B11*(1 + B2)
13	7	= B12*(1 + B2)
14	8	= B13*(1 + B2)
15	9	= B14*(1 + B2)
16	10	= B15*(1 + B2)

Figure 7.24   (a) Screen display (b) Actual cell reference

3 A new car depreciates in value each year. That is, the value of the car decreases by a certain percentage. Set up a spreadsheet that includes a cell for the original value of the car, the depreciation rate and the value of the car after each year for six years. Start with a car of value £15,000 and a depreciation rate of 25 per cent. Remember to use an absolute value when referring to the cell with the depreciation rate.

Printing your spreadsheet

Small spreadsheets are easily printed on one page of paper. However, large spreadsheets may take several sheets of paper and care must be taken to ensure they are printed out in the correct order and that breaks are in appropriate places. Most spreadsheets have a print preview option which allows a display of everything to be printed on the screen. This is very useful for ensuring page breaks are in the correct place.

Most spreadsheet programs allow a lot of flexibility in printing. They usually allow you to print your spreadsheet across the widest part of the page. Other options commonly available are printing with or without gridlines and printing with or without row and column headings. Headers and footers displaying page numbers, date, time, document title and other information may also be included.

Charting with a spreadsheet

Cells of the spreadsheet may be selected and a chart created by the program. These charts are very useful for displaying information. The common forms of spreadsheet charts are:

◆ bar charts   ◆ column charts   ◆ line charts   ◆ pie charts

all of which can be shown in 2'D' or 3'D'.

The spreadsheet in Figure 7.25 tracks the average price of a popular share for six months. (Note: share prices are normally shown in pence per share. Therefore 436 per share means £4.36.)

	A	B	C
1	Average Share Price for ABC plc		
2	Jan-96	136	
3	Feb-96	152	
4	Mar-96	168	
5	Apr-96	144	
6	May-96	101	
7	Jun-96	83	

Figure 7.25   Share price spreadsheet (monthly average price for ordinary shares in ABC plc.)

These share prices can be presented on a line graph as shown in Figure 7.26.

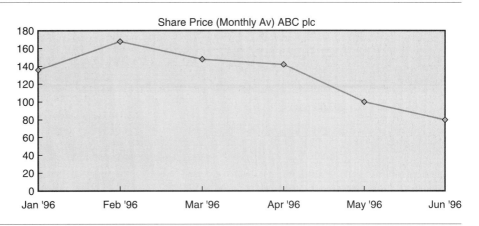

Figure 7.26 Line graph charting share prices

Note that the levels for the horizontal and vertical axes are generated by the spreadsheet program.

Pie charts are useful for representing data such as a budget so that the contribution of each item to the whole can be seen.

A pie chart of these figures could be produced by carrying out the following steps.

- Highlight the cells of the spreadsheet to be used, that is A1 to B5.
- Choose the command or icon to draw a chart.
- Select the option from the gallery of charts to draw a pie chart.
- Add an appropriate title in a larger font size using the text icon.
- Save the chart.

The result should look something like Figure 7.27 which shows the cost of going to the cinema on a 3-D pie chart.

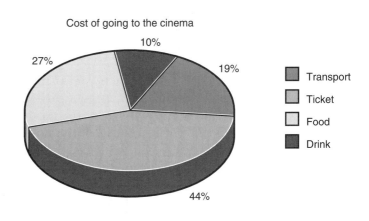

Figure 7.27 Pie chart showing the cost of going to the cinema

Bar charts are useful for making comparisons. For example, Figure 7.28 compares the costs of going to the cinema and going to a football match. Note the addition of a legend at the top of the chart, created using the correct icon or selected from menu.

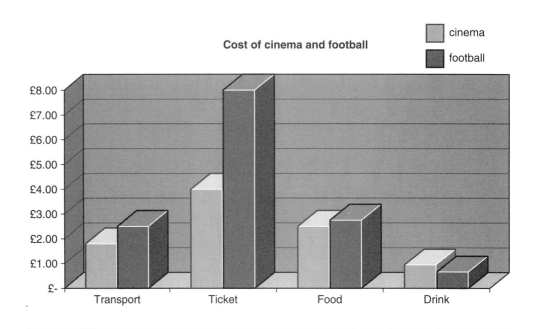

Figure 7.28   3D bar chart comparing the cost of going to the cinema and a football match

Your turn

1 Use the figures on the preceding pages to create spreadsheets and draw the charts shown in Figures 7.26, 7.27 and 7.28. In each case, alter the figures and note the changes to the charts.

2 Collect the prices of ten different items in two competing supermarkets. Enter the prices on a spreadsheet and use a bar chart to show the comparison.

Review questions

1 What is meant by the term 'active cell'? How do you know which cell is the active cell?

2 How many different ways are there to move the cursor around the spreadsheet you use? Write down each of these methods.

3 What is meant by 'what if' analysis. Give two examples where this type of analysis would be useful.

4 Explain the difference between a relative reference and an absolute reference. When would an absolute reference be used?

Tasks

1 Use a spreadsheet to work out the cost of purchasing a personal computer for use at home. You should include the cost of the computer itself, additional drives, monitor, printer, system software and integrate software package.

2 Create a spreadsheet to work out the profit for a month's trading of a service station. The income is made up of petrol and oil sales of £39,563, £13,450 labour charges of and spare parts sales of £4503. The expenses are made up of salaries of £12,000, rent of £6500 and the cost of goods (petrol, oil, spare parts) being £19,766.

3 Compile a list of 15 different items that can be purchased at a supermarket. Use a spreadsheet to list the items. Find out the prices of the items from two different supermarkets, enter them on the spreadsheet and compare the total price.

4 Create a spreadsheet to work out the annual salaries of employees of a company following a pay rise. Use cell A3 to contain the pay rise percentage and use an absolute reference in the formula you create. Try the spreadsheet with the following figures:

Surname	Initials	Old Salary	New Salary
Carey	P.J.	£35500	
Peters	R.F.	£23000	
Rowland	K.M.	£43555	
Cobb	J.J.	£18434	

5 Create a spreadsheet that can be used to work out the value of a house if it increases at a steady rate for a number of years.

   Assume that the house is purchased for £125000 and that it increases in value by 2 per cent every year. The spreadsheet should show the value of the house at the end of every year.

   a How much would the house be worth after 10 years?

   b How much would it be worth if it increased in value by 5 per cent each year?

6 The owner of Anita's Auto Rental estimates the expenses for a year as follows:

Wages	£125000
Rent	£34000
Advertising	£58000
Insurance	£37500
Interest	£4500
Electricity	£21000
Telephone	£5600
Postage	£3450
Printing	£4550
Stationery	£3250
Repairs/Servicing	£6750

Create a spreadsheet to work out the total of the expenses. What happens to the total if:

◆ the wages are increased by 2 per cent

◆ all other expenses are increased by 5 per cent.

7 Investigate the use of functions in the spreadsheet you use. How many functions are available for use? How do you think they might be useful?

8 Select a company from the listings of the stock market and follow its share price for two weeks. Enter the prices on a spreadsheet and use a suitable chart to represent the information.

Databases

8

What is a database?

Data consists of recorded facts, figures, images and sounds about people, objects, events or many other items. Data is collected and stored in a database. A database is made up of data which is arranged so that it can be looked at, organised and selected, as shown in Figure 8.1. Each item of data is related to each other item in some way. A database stores data that has some use to the person or persons who established the database.

Databases are used to provide information at home and in business. Some examples of databases are:

- a telephone directory
- the names of students who attend a school
- video titles in a video library
- employees in a company
- passengers on an airline flight
- records of births kept by a Local Registrar of Births, Deaths and Marriages.

Nasser Younis
101 Station Road
SOUTHEND-ON-SEA
SS1 3JT

(01702) 551264

Donald Gilroy
179 Old School Lane
BALLYCLARE
County Antrim
BJ39 9GT

(01960) 743612.

Jennifer McCallam
107 Church Street
LOSSIEMOUTH
Morayshire
N31 6ER

(01343) 812593

Figure 8.1   A database of names, addresses and telephone numbers on cards

Why do we have databases?

Data on its own is not very useful. It needs to be organised and interpreted so that it has meaning. Sorting data helps make the data easy to interpret.

People use databases to find information about goods, services and other people.

Organisations use databases to provide information that helps when people are making decisions. Many organisations need databases to carry out their day to day business.

Examples – Databases kept by individuals

People create databases for use at home or for their own personal use. The database may be stored on a computer or written in a book or on cards. Some examples are:

- telephone numbers in a teledex
- a list of valuable items that are kept at home
- an atlas which is used for reference
- a dictionary
- a collection of cooking recipes
- a list of names and addresses for Christmas cards.

Examples – Databases kept by organisations

Businesses and organisations create and maintain databases as part of their everyday operation. These organisations use databases:

- a school keeps a database of all its students' names, addresses and telephone numbers
- a supermarket has a database of all the items that it sells
- a bank has a database of all its customers and their accounts
- local libraries keep catalogues of books that are lent out
- a tennis club keeps a database of its members
- a video library uses a database to keep track of both its customers and its videotape.

There are businesses which create databases and then sell information to other businesses and organisations:

- credit rating for people applying for a loan
- lists of suitable names for direct mail advertising

Your turn

1 Think of the databases that you use at home and at school. These databases may be stored on a computer or may be written in a book or on cards. For this exercise, it does not matter how they are stored.
   a List five different databases that you use at home.
   b List five different databases that you have your name recorded on at school.
2 List five different databases that are used by organisations that you come into contact with outside school.
3 You have been asked to keep track of the members of a local sports club and you have to create a database. Write down what information you think you would want to get from your database. What information would you need to keep?

The telephone directory

The telephone directory is a database. It stores names, addresses and telephone numbers for a large number of people and organisations (these are called subscribers). The entries in the telephone book are sorted alphabetically and split into two sections: Business Numbers and Residential Numbers.

Four typical entries in the telephone book are:

◆ Pollards Pork Pies, 4-6 Mill Ln, Banbury   750724
◆ Webbs Coaches, The Green, Evenley   702598
◆ Arnold F, 93 Parsons Cl, Silverstone   859423
◆ Hyde K, 4 Church View, Bicester   248485

Large organisations can now purchase copies of the entire country telephone directory stored on CD ROM.

Your turn

1 Refer to your current telephone directory.
  a What is the first name in the Residential Numbers section?
  b What is the last name in the Business Numbers section?
  c How often does your surname occur in the directory?
2 OXCHOL is a database containing the details of individuals affected during the cholera epidemic in Oxford in 1854. Each of 317 individuals affected were given a unique 'Case' number. Figure 8.2 shows part of the records of 9 'cases'. Answer the questions below by referring to Figure 8.2.
  a How many 'cases' were in the parish St Ebbe?
  b How many 'cases' were female?
  c How old was 'case' 6 the tailor?

CASE	DATE	SEX	AGE	OCCUPATION	PARISH	RESULT
2	Aug 12	F	45	Charwoman	St Ebbe	Recovery
6	Aug 29	F	34	Tailor	St Ebbe	Recovery
7	Aug 30	M	9	Carter's son	St Ebbe	Recovery
9	Aug 30	F	19	Butcher's daughter	St Ebbe	Recovery
10	Aug 30	F	4	Soldier's daughter	St Ebbe	Recovery
11	Aug 30	M	40	Labourer	St Ebbe	Recovery
12	Aug 30	M	30	Railway porter	St Thomas	Recovery
15	Sep 1	F	40	Charwoman	St Ebbe	Recovery
40	Sep 7	M	33	Coal merchant	St Thomas	Recovery

Figure 8.2 OXCHOL – part of a database recording victims of the 1854 cholera epidemic in Oxford

3 Figure 8.3 below shows the top 15 most watched TV shows for the week beginning 26 June 1995.

POSITION	SHOW	MILLIONS	CHANNEL
1	EastEnders (Thurs/Sun)	15.72	BBC1
2	Coronation Street (Mon/Wed)	15.42	ITV
3	The National Lottery Live	11.01	BBC1
4	Neighbours (Mon)	10.62	BBC1
5	Emmerdale (Tue/Thur)	9,87	ITV
6	Wycliffe	9.71	ITV
7	Bramwell	9.62	ITV
8	Home & Away (Mon)	9.31	ITV
9	The Bill (Fri)	9.19	ITV
10	Fawlty Towers	9.16	BBC1
11	Birds of a Feather	9.07	BBC1
12	Men Behaving Badly	8.12	BBC1
13	News/Sport (Sat 8.45)	8.05	BBC1
14	Surprise, Surprise	7.99	ITV
15	A Touch of Frost	7.85	ITV

Figure 8.3   Top TV shows *Source; BARB/RSMB*

a How many of the top 15 TV programmes were shown on ITV?
b How many viewers did the top TV programme have?
c How many of the top TV programmes were not soaps?
d How many of the top 15 TV programmes were 'factual'?

Why use a computer for a database?

Computers are used for databases because they:

- can store large amounts of data
- can find and display data quickly
- can be updated or changed quickly
- they allow data to be searched and presented in a variety of useful ways
- summaries of data can be easily obtained
- make the data available in many different locations
- allow for data to be transferred easily
- allow a large number of people to use the database at the same time.

What makes up a database?

A database is made up of a collection of files about somebody, something or an entity. An *entity* is a person or object about which information needs to be recorded.

Each entity that is used in a database is given a name. Many databases consist of only one entity. The telephone book contains data about people and organisations called subscribers. Therefore the entity used in the telephone book could be called a subscriber.

Each piece of information about an entity is called a record. For example, a subscriber whose last name is 'Paul' has the following data stored as a record in the telephone directory: Paul T J, 59 Highfield Rd., Cromer 01263 76142

A record is made up of a number of separate pieces of data. Each of these pieces is called a field. Each field is given a name so that it may be recognised. In the telephone book, the record is made up of the fields called last name, initials, street, town, telephone number – see Figure 8.4.

Field name	Data for each field
Last name	Paul
Initials	T. J.
Street	59 Highfield Road
Town	Cromer
Telephone number	01263 761422

Figure 8.4 The record for the subscriber Paul T.J.

The field 'last name' has the value 'Paul', the field 'initials' has the value 'T.J.' and so on.

Example

The OXCHOL database uses an entity called 'Cases' which is made up of fields called: Date, Sex, Occupation, Parish, Result.

Your turn

1 Write down the field names used in the following database (Figure 8.5) which stores the names and addresses of people.

	Given Name	Last Name	Title	Address	Town/City	County	Post code
1	Tracy	Dillon	Ms	14 Station Rd.	Sidmouth	Devon	EX10 8YL
2	Joanne	Turner	Ms	670 New North Rd.	Ilford	Essex	IG7 3HT
3	Peter	Cox	Mr	67 Church Lane	Thirsk	N. Yorks	YO7 2JP
4	John	Hall	Mr	97 Orchard Cres.	Coventry	Warks	CV3 6PJ
5	Alan	Walters	Mr	73 Hilton Rd.	Leeds	Yorks	LS8 4HJ

Figure 8.5 Address database

2 Figure 8.6 shows one address on an address database. Write down the field names used in this database.

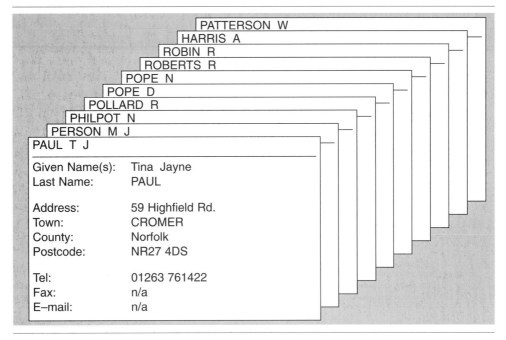

Figure 8.6   Address database

3 Write down the field names used in UK's most watched TV programmes database in Figure 8.3.
4 Figure 8.7 below shows one record from a database of runs scored in cricket text matches. Write down the field names used in this database. How is the value in the field called 'Average' worked out?

PLAYER:	Gooch, G. A.
DEBUT:	'75-'76
MATCHES:	113
INNINGS:	206
NOT OUT:	6
HIGHEST:	333
RUNS:	8655
100's:	20
AVERAGE:	43.49

Figure 8.7   Graham Gooch's record on a database of test cricket aggregate runs

5 For the database in Questions 1 to 4, write down the name of the entity about which data is being stored.

Accessing a database

A database needs to be accessed to be of any use. The particular parts of the database that are wanted can be selected. Each database software package has its own way of finding the wanted data.

For example, a typical query is looking up a name in the telephone directory and finding the telephone number. You will need to know the last name and, perhaps, the initials and at least some of the address. Finding a telephone number is a search of the database.

Each database language makes queries in different ways. A typical query made from a telephone book might be:

FIND ALL SUBSCRIBERS WITH LAST NAME = 'Paul' AND INITIALS = 'T.J'.

A query or search of the database is made up of the following things:

◆ the field or fields to be used to make the selection – for example, 'last name'

◆ the operator that is used for the selection – for example, =.

◆ the value or values that are to be looked for – for example, 'Paul'

In Microsoft Works, records are selected by choosing the value for comparison. It is possible to locate all records which match a single or range of criteria by applying query. To do this 'query' is selected from the view menu. By entering the criteria by each field and then selecting 'list' all those which match will be displayed. If you wanted to list all with a last name beginning with 'A' you would enter 'A*' in field last name. If you wanted to locate all batsmen with averages greater than 50 you would enter '>50' in the average field.

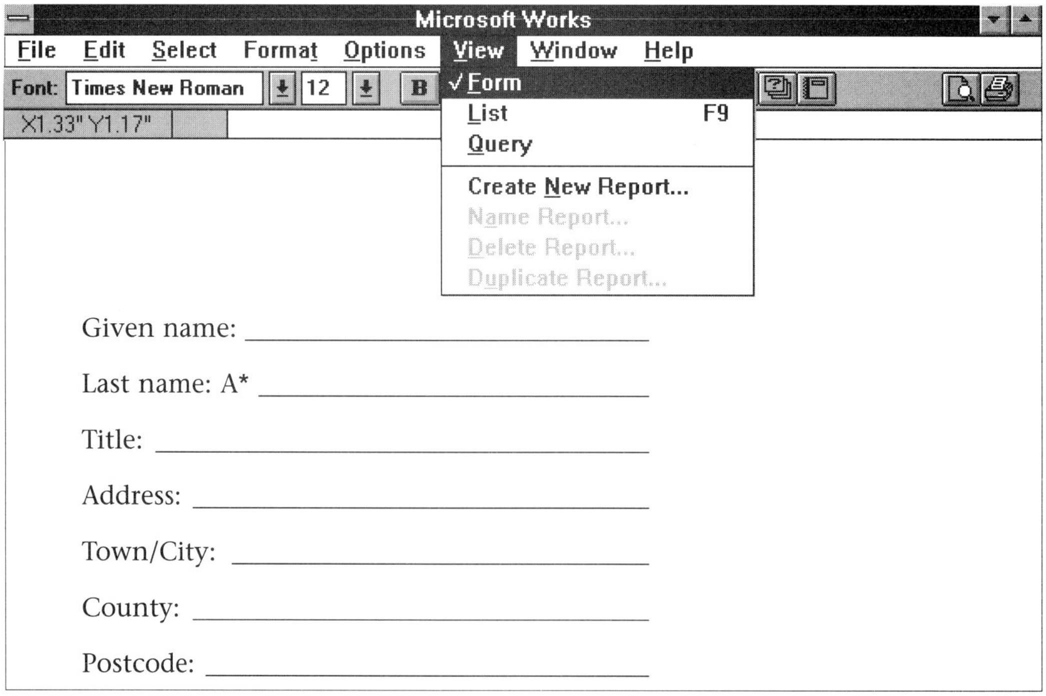

Figure 8.8 Making a selection from a database – choosing all records last name begins with A

Your turn

1 Figure 8.9 (below) shows the batting averages for the 15 leading scorers in Test cricket.
   a How many players had averages greater than 50? Who were they?
   b Which players had made at least one score of greater than 300?
   c Which players has scored more than 8000 runs?
   d How many players had played less than 100 Test matches?
   e How many players were English?
   f Which player had the highest average?

Player	Country	Matches	Innings	Not outs	Highest	Runs	Average
Border, A R	Australia	156	265	44	205	11,174	50.56
Gavaskar, S M	India	125	214	16	236	10,122	51.12
Miandad, Javed	Pakistan	124	189	21	280	8,832	52.57
Gooch, G A	England	111	201	6	333	8,564	43.92
Richards, I V A	West Indies	121	182	12	291	8,540	50.24
Gower, D I	England	117	204	18	215	8,231	44.25
Boycott, G	England	109	193	23	246	8,114	47.73
Sobers, G S	West Indies	93	160	21	365	8,032	57.78
Cowdrey, M C	England	115	188	15	182	7,624	44.07
Greenidge, C G	West Indies	108	185	16	226	7,558	44.72
Lloyd, C H	West Indies	110	175	14	242	7,515	46.68
Haynes, D L	West Indies	116	202	25	184	7,487	42.30
Hammond, W R	England	85	140	16	336	7,249	58.46
Chappel, G S	Australia	88	151	19	247	7,110	53.86
Bradman, D G	Australia	52	80	10	334	6,996	99.94

Figure 8.9 Batting averages for some Text match cricket players

Why change a database?

A database is only useful if the data it contains is correct and up to date.

A new telephone book is published every year. As people change house, have new telephones connected or old numbers disconnected, the directory is altered. B.T. Directory Enquiries keeps an up to date list of all the changes. Making changes to the data is called updating the database.

Databases are updated at various intervals, depending upon the nature of the database. The telephone directory for each area is printed every year. It is always out of date to some extent.

The stock exchange carries out its trading of shares using computers. Its database is updated on-line, that is, as soon as the transaction takes place. Enquiries to the stock exchange database reflect the latest up to date information. These are both examples of data which is sold.

What changes are made to the data in a database?

Three types of changes are made to the data in a database. These are:

◆ adding new records   ◆ deleting records   ◆ altering records.

Each of these types of changes needs to be made regularly and promptly.

Examples

The telephone directory might make changes in the following circumstances:

◆ adding new records – a new subscriber is added to the telephone network
◆ altering records – a subscriber changes address and/or telephone number

◆ deleting a record – a subscriber decides not to continue with the service; an organisation closes down and no longer needs a telephone.

A school might make changes in the following ways:

◆ adding new records – a new student in enrolled in the school
◆ deleting a record – a student has left the school and is not likely to return

◆ altering records – a student changes his or her address.

Deletions are done with a great deal of care. The accuracy of the database depends upon records being deleted when they are no longer of use.

Altering records must also be carried out with care. It is important that the record being altered is the correct one – that is, it must be uniquely identified. Large databases such as those kept by British Telecom will have many subscribers with the same name and initials.

Your turn

1 Figure 8.9 (on page 105) shows the batting averages for some Test match cricketers.
   a Under what circumstances would a new player be added to the table?
   b Under what circumstances would a player be deleted from the table?
   c In which fields would the values never need to be altered?
   d In which fields would the values be altered?

	Player	Games (league)	Goals (league)	Goals (cup)	Goals (pen)	Total Goals
1	Schmeical	40				
2	Parker	39 (+1 sub)				
3	Irwin	42	2	2		4
4	Bruce	41	3	2		5
5	Kanchelskis	28 (+3 sub)	6	4		10
6	Pallister	41	1			1
7	Robson	10 (+5 sub)	1	1		2
8	Ince	39	8	1		9
9	Keane	34 (+3 sub)	5	1		6
10	Hughes	36	11	9		20
11	Giggs	32 (+6 sub)	13	4		17
12	McClair	12 (+14 sub)	1	5		6
13	Sharpe	26 (+4 sub)	9	2		11
14	Cantona	34	18	5	4	27
15	Butt	0 (+1 sub)				
16	Martin	1				
17	Phelan	1 (+1 sub)				
18	Ferguson	1 (+1 sub)				
19	Dublin	1 (=4 sub)	1	1		2
20	Thornley	0 (+1 sub)				
21	Walsh	2(+1 sub)				
22	Neville	1				
23	McKee	1				

Figure 8.10   Manchester United Football Club players records 1994-5 Record

2 Look at the table showing the 1994-5 record of the Manchester United
   football team and answer the following questions.
   a How many goals in total did Cantona score during the 1994-5 season?
      If he had scored one more goal in the F.A. Cup which field or fields
      might need to be changed?
   b Which fields would not need to be altered during the season?
   c When would a player be deleted or added to the database?
   d In which fields would the values never need to be changed?
   e What changes would need to be made at the start of each season?
3 Look at the chart of most watched TV programmes (on page 101) and
   answer the following questions.
   a How often would the chart need to be updated?
   b If the most watched TV programme (East Enders) maintains its position
      for the following week, what changes would be made to the values of the
      fields for that record?
   d When would a TV programme be deleted from the database?

Sorting a database

The data in a database may be sorted in ascending or descending order based on any one field (or more) that makes up the records in the database. The field that is used to sort the database is called the key field. Key fields are used to identify records in a database. Usually, each record has a key field which uniquely identifies that record.

Ascending order means going from smallest to largest. Names in the telephone directory are arranged in ascending order.

Descending order means going from largest to smallest. Teams on a league table are usually arranged in descending order – for example, the Premier Football League table. This is achieved by selecting 'Sort Records' in the Select menu and then whichever field you wish to make the key field.

Example – Name and address database

The name and address database in Figure 8.5 (on page 102) can be sorted in ascending order on the last name – Figure 8.11.

	A	B	C	D	E	F	G
1	**Given Name**	**Last Name**	**Title**	**Address**	**Town/City**	**County**	**Postcode**
2	Peter	Cox	Mr	67 Church Lane	Thirsk	N. Yorks	YO7 2JP
3	Tracy	Dillon	Ms	14 Station Rd.	Sidmouth	Devon	EX10 8YL
4	John	Hall	Mr	97 Orchard Cres.	Coventry	Warks	CV3 6PJ
5	Joanne	Turner	Ms	670 New North Rd.	Ilford	Essex	IG7 3HT
6	Alan	Walters	Mr	73 Hilton Rd.	Leeds	Yorks	LS8 4HJ

Figure 8.11   Names and addresses sorted on the field 'Surname'

	A	B	C	D	E	F	G
1	**Given Name**	**Last Name**	**Title**	**Address**	**Town/City**	**County**	**Postcode**
2	John	Hall	Mr	97 Orchard Cres.	Coventry	Warks	CV3 6PJ
3	Tracy	Dillon	Ms	14 Station Rd.	Sidmouth	Devon	EX10 8YL
4	Joanne	Turner	Ms	670 New North Rd.	Ilford	Essex	IG7 3HT
5	Alan	Walters	Mr	73 Hilton Rd.	Leeds	Yorks	LS8 4HJ
6	Peter	Cox	Mr	67 Church Lane	Thirsk	N. Yorks	YO7 2JP

Figure 8.12   Names and addresses sorted in ascending order on the field 'Postcode'

What is a report?

An important use for a database is the generation of reports. Reports provide information for the user. This usually involves making a selection from the database and then arranging it in a manner that is easy to understand. A report will normally only show the values from some of the fields in each record. It also often includes the totals of certain fields that will provide summary information for the user.

Example – OXCHOL Database

Look back to the OXCHOL database fig 8.2. This shows nine records from the 317 on the database of victims of the 1854 cholera epidemic in Oxford. The nine cases here all recovered. If I wished to write a REPORT on say the Average age of female victims who survived this would be easily achieved by

1st step: Selecting all female records by applying a query by selecting query in the View menu – Field Sex: F

2nd Step: Selecting Create New Report in the View menu and then appropriate fields – including Age and then the appropriate Report Statistics (Average Age).

The report function allows you to include a title and alter the presentation of the final report by grouping sections of information. The final report is shown in figure 8.13 below.

Age of women in OXCHOL database			
Case	**Date**	**Sex**	**Age**
2	06/08	F	45
6	06/08	F	34
9	30/08	F	19
10	30/08	F	4
15	01/09	F	40
			AVG:
			28.4

Figure 8.13

Your turn

1 Figure 8.14 is part of a database of customers for a department store. They show the customer's names, the value of their purchases and the department where the purchases were made. Create a database using these figures and then sort and report to discover:

a How many of the purchases were made on 22 January 96. What their total value is.

Last name	First name	Purchase value	Date	Department
Braun	Jacob	£450	12 Jan 1996	Sports
Brencic	Kate	£345	22 Jan 1996	Sports
Brencic	Kate	£21	23 Jan 1966	Book
Brencic	Kate	£35	4 Feb 1996	Clothing
Byrne	Marianne	£59	31 Jan 1996	Cookware
Cefai	Desmond	£78	5 Jan 1996	Book
Cook	Russell	£475	12 Jan 1996	Sports
Cook	Russell	£429	26 Jan 1996	Clothing
Denaro	Paula	£335	22 Jan 1996	Cookware
Denaro	Paula	£89	1 Feb 1996	Clothing
Femino	Jana	£24	12 Jan 1996	Book
Giacomelli	Sam	£87	13 Jan 1996	Book
Giacomelli	Sam	£37	27 Jan 1996	Cookware
Hudson	Sandra	£44	2 Feb 1996	Book
Saunders	William	£284	12 Jan 1996	Clothing

Figure 8.14   Customer purchases

b How many purchases were made in the Book Department. What their total value is.

c How the database is sorted. Sort in two other ways that might be useful.

d Generate two different reports with sub-totals that might be useful.

2 All schools keep their student records on a database. These records include name and address, telephone number, date of birth, tutor group, emergency contact, Doctor plus a range of other data that they find useful.

a List the type of data that you think your school would keep about you on a database.

b Which parts of the data you identified in (a) do you think the following groups of people should be able to see about you: principal or head teacher; teachers not teaching you; teachers who teach you; your parents; you; other students.

The Data Protection Act 1984

Any organisation which holds personal information on computer about employees, customers, patients, pupils or students who are living and can be identified from this data must:

◆ register with the Data Protection Registrar details of the data stored and the uses to which it is put

◆ follow certain rules about how it can be used and protect it, using adequate security systems.

Individual citizens who have data about them stored in this way have certain rights. These include the right to see and be given a copy of any personal details held. The data must be deleted once its purpose has been fulfilled.

Creating a database

In business, designing and creating a database is a complex process and it comes after a lot of analysis.

The following are typical issues that need to be worked out.

◆ What is the entity about which data will be collected?

◆ What data about the entity needs to be collected?

◆ Which pieces of data are going to be used for searching and sorting?

◆ How can each different record in the database be uniquely identified?

◆ What information will need to be retrieved from the database?

Creating and using a small database involved the same steps.

◆ Identify the entity that is going to be used in the database. That is, identify the person or thing about which you are going to store data. You also need to know what results you expect to get from your database.

◆ Define the database by identifying the fields that will make up each record.

◆ Enter the initial data into the database.

◆ Check that the data is correct. This can be done by printing out some of the records and checking them against the original documents.

◆ Work out reports and searches that will be used often.

◆ Modify the database as required.

◆ Back up the database regularly by making copies of it and storing the copies in a safe place.

Your turn

Create a database to keep track of members of any school club or team. The database will need to include members' names and addresses as well as their age (this is needed for under-age competitions).

- The entity to be used is member, with the fields as requested. It is written: member (last name, first name, address, town/village, postcode, age).
- The database is defined using a database management package. Each field will need to be defined using the names, making sure they are meaningful. Each field can be defined as text or a number. In this case, all the fields except age are text.
- Now enter the data. See Figure 8.15 for a sample database.
- Check the data carefully. Look at each record in turn and compare it to the original data. Make any necessary changes.
- Make sure at least one copy of the database is copied to another disk and stored in a safe place. Backups should be carried out whenever the database is altered.
- It can be useful to have standard reports and searches saved. Most database management systems allow some of the sorts and searches to be pre-defined. One useful report might be to produce mailing labels.
- If a database is to be of use its definition will need to be modified. That is, in time new fields will have to be added and some fields may become of no use. More or different information will need to be stored. In this example, the addition of a telephone number for the member of the club would be useful. The database management package should allow the creation of new fields such as this.

	A	B	C	D	E
1	**Last Name**	**Given Name**	**Address**	**Town/City**	**Postcode**
2	Aleksic	Joe	6 Jeffrey Avenue	Banbury	OX16 7NW
3	Cheung	Gill	16 Rebecca Rd	Banbury	OX15 6TE
4	Green	Keith	3 Hope St.	Bicester	OX12 5LT
5	Cowen	Pam	23 Nepean Ave	Banbury	OX16 8PV
6	Druzic	Jane	150 Victoria Rd	Bicester	OX12 4RT

Figure 8.15 Database of junior sports team/club

 # Review questions

1 Define these terms: field, record and file.
2 Why is it important to back up a database?
3 How often should a database be updated? Explain, using an example of a database.
4 What is a key field in a database? How is it used when sorting records?
5 What does the term 'report' mean when considering a database?
6 What is involved in a search of a database?
7 What steps need to be taken to create a database?
8 Explain the difference between data and information.

9 Give four reasons why businesses now use computers rather than paper files to store data.

 # Tasks

1 Design a database to track customers for a small business. Enter fifteen imaginary customers with their name, address, telephone and facsimile numbers. Produce a set of mailing labels for the customer file.

2 Design a database of employees. What information would be needed? Create a form to collect that information together with anything else of use. Create ten imaginary employees for the database.

3 Video Plus Direct is a business organisation which specialises in selling video and audio-cassettes to customers direct by post. They maintain a database of every video title still in print 15,000 video titles and 2500 audio-cassettes. Trained operators can search by titles, stars and directors. They can give a brief account of any title, together with availability, price, running time, certificate and year of production.
   a Design your own video database which contains the same fields as the Video Plus Direct database.
   b Can you suggest any other useful fields
   c Ask each member of your class/team to collect and enter information from videos they own.
   d When the class database is complete produce a number of different reports, e.g. titles of videos with the same male/female lead.

4 PC Globe is a database made up of data about countries around the world. It contains statistics about 190 different countries. The data is accessed using a computer. There is also a Macintosh version. Use your school's latest version or any other computer based atlas to find:
   a What the population of America is. What the projected population for the year 2000 is.
   b What the area of America is.
   c What the life expectancy of both males and females in the UK is.
   d What the four largest cities in the UK and what the populations are.
   e What the average maximum temperature in Birmingham in August is.

9 Desktop Publishing

What is desktop publishing?

Desktop publishing (DTP) refers to the use of a computer system to create a publication that is ready for printing. This includes entering text, creating and placing graphics and combining them into a report, document or magazine. Figure 9.1 shows the steps in the publishing process.

Before the use of computers, the task of laying out a publication was largely carried out by hand. Each page of a publication was manually cut and pasted up using a large paste board. The computer enables this entire process to be carried out at the desktop.

Typical hardware includes a:

◆ computer, often with a large screen monitor
◆ printer – usually laser printer or ink jet printer for high quality output
◆ scanner, for scanning photographs and other images.

Printer (right), scanner (left), and computer (middle) make up a typical desktop publishing system

 Your turn

Find out which publications your school produces using desktop publishing. Answer the following questions.

    a What are the names of the publications?
    b How often are they published?
    c Who does the layout for each publication?

d What type of computers are used for the layout?
e What type of printer is used?
f What software is used in the production of each publication?
g Where is the final document printed?

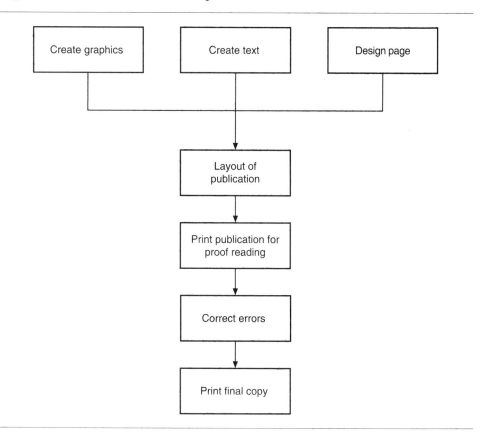

Figure 9.1   The publishing process

Microsoft Publisher

Microsoft Publisher is a page layout program that can help in the design of:

- ◆ signs
- ◆ banners
- ◆ letterheads
- ◆ greeting cards.
- ◆ business stationery

It has sample layouts for each of these types of documents and also includes a large range of graphic elements that can be used. Figure 9.2 shows a menu for the production of a range of standard document, these are referred to as 'Wizards'.

Creating your own letterhead

To create your own letterhead using Microsoft Publisher you would:

- ◆ create a logo in a graphics program
- ◆ open the Publisher template for letterhead and bring in your own logo to replace the default graphic included in the letterhead
- ◆ enter and/or place text in the appropriate positions. The top of the letterhead includes a logo and text giving information about the business name.

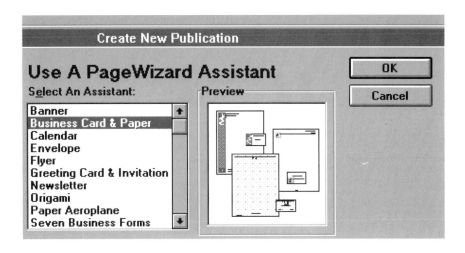

Figure 9.2 Menu for stationery - a reduced view

To make your own letterhead, the logo can be imported from a graphics program and placed into the document or you can use clip art. To do this, copy the logo to the clipboard and then paste it into the letterhead using the Edit menu. The publishing packages takes you through all the stages required to produce the document using simple questions about style. The fonts and font size can be adjusted from the Font menu. Figure 9.3 below shows the Business Card from Microsoft Publisher with the logo produced in Chapter 6 and new information about the company added.

Figure 9.3 A Business card placed onto letterhead

At the bottom of the letterhead a text block was added – that is, telephone and facsimile number.

The final result is shown in a reduced view in Figure 9.4.

Figure 9.4 The letterhead

Your turn

1 Examine your school's printed letterhead.
    a Where is the name of the school?
    b Is there a school logo on the letterhead? If so, where is it placed?
    c Where is the address of the school?
    d Where are the telephone and facsimile numbers for the school?
    e Is there anything else on the letterhead? If so, what is it and where is it placed?
2 Examine three other pieces of printed letterhead and answer questions 1 a to 1 e with regard to them.
3 Use Microsoft Publisher or any other page layout software, to design, save and print:
    a your own business letterhead
    b an invitation to your birthday party
    c an advertising poster for a car boot sale.

In each case you should use the ready made examples provided by Microsoft Publisher. Once these have been successfully created, import your own graphics, or use an appropriate clip art image.

The publishing process

The publishing process involves the bringing together of text and graphics on a page using a computer.

The sources of graphics are:

- photographs
- artwork created by someone for a publication
- clip art
- character modification packages, eg. Microsoft Word-art
- elements such as lines and boxes created within the layout program.

Each of the graphic images must be in a form that can be used by the computer.

The page design is created using page layout software, after a sketch has been done using pen and paper.

The page layout software is used to combine the various elements into a publication.

How important is design for a successful publication?

To create an effective publication, design principles and typography are important.

The purpose of any publication is clear communication. How it is said is just as important as what is said. Hence, graphic design is a key element in an effective magazine. Effective graphic design leads the reader through the publication.

A successful publication is one that:

- is easy to read
- has a clear purpose that is reflected in the text and the design
- has graphic elements that are relevant
- has a logical sequence of direction through the document – most people scan a page from top left to bottom right
- has page to page consistency throughout the document.

Your turn

1 Look at some publications in your school library. Write down the features in each publication that you think make the publication easy to read and those which make the publication difficult to read.
2 For each of the publications you looked at in Question 1, write down the main purpose of the publication.

What does page layout software do?

Page layout software is used to design and layout the pages of a document. A document can be a single page advertisement leaflet, a business card, an invitation, a four page newsletter, a magazine of many pages or a book. Page layout software is concerned with the arrangement of text and graphics on a page. Many magazines and newsletters are produced using computers and page layout software.

Figure 9.5 shows a standard first page for a newsletter produced using Aldus PageMaker. It includes the following elements:

- logo
- the name of the publication
- a photograph
- a second level headline
- body text
- room for a photograph.

It has three columns for text.

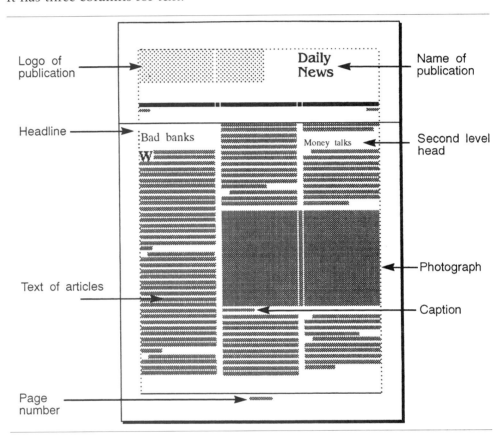

Figure 9.5 A sample page of a newsletter produced using Aldus PageMaker

Your turn

1 Look at page 3 of this book and answer the following questions,
   a What is the main heading?
   b How many columns of text are there on the page?
   c Are there any photographs on the page? If so, where are they placed? Are there any other diagrams on the page? If so, what are they?
   d Are there any lines drawn on the page? If so, where are they? Why do you think they were put there?
2 Examine the first page of a student newspaper or newsletter from your school.
   a Write down where the following appear and what they are: logo; headline; second level headlines; photographs; drawings; lines and boxes; page numbers; table of contents.
   b How many columns of text does it have?

3 Repeat Question 2, but this time look at other student newspapers and newsletters that are in your school library.

4 Examine single page advertising leaflets that come into your home. Write down the main purpose of each of these leaflets. What do they do to grab your attention?

When not to use a word processor

Word processors offer some of the features of a desktop publishing package. However, it is generally more difficult to work in columns, to manipulate and move graphic images and to create master pages in word processing programs.

If a document is text-based and does not require graphics, then a word processor is the most appropriate package to use to produce the document.

Design and layout

The design and layout of a document will determine:

◆ how easy the document is to read
◆ the impact the document makes on the reader
◆ how successfully the reader understands the message of the of the document.

The intended audience influences design decision. An end of year school magazine would be designed and laid out differently from a leaflet advertising a rock concert.

The person using the desktop publishing software will determine the:

◆ number of text columns per page
◆ size and style of the body text
◆ size and style of the heading text
◆ amount of white space on a page
◆ position of graphics and photographs.

Some basic rules of desktop publishing

Although there is no `right` way to set out a publication there are some general rules that can be applied. For example:

◆ Serif fonts are generally easier to read than sans serif fonts. A document with a large amount of text should be designed so that the body of the text is printed in a serif font such as Times New Roman or New Century Schoolbook.
◆ Text in capitals is difficult to read and should be avoided.

◆ Sans serif fonts are suitable for headlines and advertisements or in display boxes.
◆ Text should be left justified.
◆ Lines of text should not be too long as this makes it difficult to read – around 30 to 40 characters per line is a good guide.

Your turn

Look at a free newspaper in your town and answer the following questions.

a How many columns are there on each page? Does this vary throughout the newspaper?

b Where are the photographs placed throughout the paper (top right, bottom left, etc.)?

c Are the headlines printed in upper case only or a mixture of upper and lower case?

d Is the font used for the headlines a serif or a sans serif font?

Designing your publication - what is a grid?

A grid is used to create the structure of each page. It consists of a series of lines that divide the page. The grid shows how many columns are being used, the width of the margins – both top and bottom – and the space between columns. The structure that the grid creates is very important in helping to produce an effective publication.

Page layout software offers the opportunity to design a publication with almost any type of grid for setting out the elements. Looking at magazines, newspapers and books can give ideas about the grid design that is most suitable for your own publication.

Single column grid

A single column grid is the simplest to work with and very useful for one page newsletters or advertising leaflets. It is particularly suitable for those publications that do not have a large amount of text. However, it is very limiting in terms of layout. A large font size is needed and plenty of space will have to be added to help readability. It is difficult to place graphics on the page and still get an effective publication. Figure 9.7 shows a single column grid.

Figure 9.7 A single column grid

Two column grid

A two column grid is used in more newsletters, books and material than a single column, but the design can be repetitive and there is often not enough white space. Again, the size of the font is limited. Graphics can be difficult to include as they should either extend across one column or across the full width of the page. Figure 9.8 shows an example of a two columns layout.

Figure 9.8   A two column grid

Three column grid

Three column grids offer more flexibility. Headlines can be extended across two or three columns and graphics can be placed more easily. A graphic generally looks better if it extends across complete columns – either one, two or three. Vertical graphics placed in a single column can be very effective. However, there can be limitations on the amount of white space available. Figure 9.9 shows an example of a page with a three column grid.

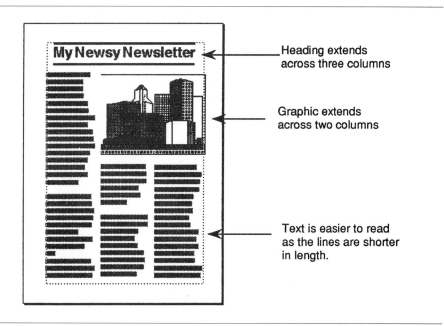

Figure 9.9   A three column grid

Other grids

Other grids can include up to seven columns, sometimes leaving a column blank to provide white space, and variable width columns. Generally, as the number of columns increases so does the flexibility of layout and the complexity of the task.

Your turn

1 Examine the free newspapers and identify the type of grid that is used.
   a How many columns are on a normal page?
   b How many columns do the photographs cover?
   c Does the number of columns vary throughout the newspaper?
2 Repeat Question 1 with:
   a your annual school or club magazine
   b two examples of weekly or monthly magazines available in your library.
3 Use a pen and paper to sketch a possible layout for a four-page class newsletter. Try both a two column grid and a three column grid.

Publication of a magazine

The steps below apply to a class newspaper of one or two A4 sides as well as to a professionally produced publication such as a monthly magazine.

First steps

The first steps are to find out:

- the audience – who is going to read the publication?
- the articles – what is going to make them interesting to read?
- purpose of the publication – why is this publication needed?
- frequency of the publication – how often will it be produced?
- time lines – when is it needed?
- printing – who will print it and what are the specifications?
- format – what will the magazine look like?

Submission of material

The material received may be:

- written pieces
- cartoons
- photographs
- illustrations.

It may be necessary to advertise that submissions are being invited; in some cases a competition could be run with a prize for the best entries.

The text may be received in the following forms:

- handwritten
- typed
- on a computer disk as a word-processed document.

How should text be prepared before layout?

To prepare text involves:

- proof-reading the article for spelling errors and correct use of grammar
- checking that the article is appropriate for the publication
- checking the length of the article – most word processors include a count of the number of words
- entering the text into a word processor if it is handwritten or typed. Good quality typed text can be entered using a scanner and optical character recognition (OCR) software
- deciding where the article should be placed.

Generally, it is better to prepare the text using a word processor. Page layout programs can recognise a range of different word processing formats.

How should graphics be prepared for desktop publishing?

To prepare a graphic involves:

- choosing images that are appropriate for the publication
- ensuring that the graphic is in a form that can be effectively reproduced
- ensuring that the graphic can be resized or cropped so that it is appropriate for the publication
- ensuring that the image enhances the publication – every image should tell a story.

Images can be imported by page layout programs, which recognise a range of different graphics formats. Images can be computer generated or created using a scanner.

Figure 9.10(a) shows a graphic image which could be imported into a page layout program. This image can be resized in proportion.

(a)  **(b)**  **(c)**

Figure 9.10   **(a)** An example of a graphic image **(b)** The same image but enlarged and cropped **(c)** The image has been distorted

The image contains the same subject matter in a different size. If required, only a part of the image can be retained. This is called `cropping`.

The retained image is different from the imported image. Figure 9.10(b) shows a resized (enlarged) and cropped image. Images can also be distorted for effect. Figure 9.10(c) shows the image from Figure 9.10(b) that has been stretched.

Your turn

Use a page layout program to import a graphic image such as clip art, scanned photograph or a piece of artwork. Do the following:
  a Resize the image without distorting it so that it goes across the whole page.
  b Resize the image and distort it by making it wider, then longer.
  c Crop the image.

A `mock up` of the publication

Before using the software to create a publication, it is useful to have a `mock up` of the finished publication. A mock up is a rough, hand–drawn sketch of the page which shows the appropriate positions of all of the important elements of the page. For example if the page size is A4 then some blank sheets of A5 paper could be folded in half to give the required number of pages. Key parts of the publication would be allocated to the appropriate page – for example, the table of contents may be on page one.

Page layout software is able to print reduced size copies of a number of pages on the one sheet of paper. These reduced size copies are called thumbnails and they can produce up to sixteen pages per sheet of paper. Thumbnails enable the designer to see what the document will look like without printing out every page. Thumbnails can also be drawn up by hand to give an idea of what the publication should look like.

Setting up a publication

A master page is used to create items that will appear on each page in a document. These items usually include:

◆ page numbering
◆ repeating text – headers and
  footers
◆ column guides
◆ graphic elements such as lines
  or a logo.

Master pages can be set up for both the left and right pages of a publication. In Figure 9.11 the pages marked `L` and `R` are master pages – what is contained on page `L` would apply to all left (even numbered) pages, that is pages 2, 4, 6, 8 and 10, and what is contained on page `R` would apply to all right (odd numbered) pages.

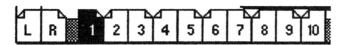

Figure 9.11 Setting up master pages

Figure 9.12 shows an example of a master page (left) which includes a two column grid, a logo, a header, a footer and a line drawn across the top of the page. Each of these elements will be repeated on every even numbered page in the document.

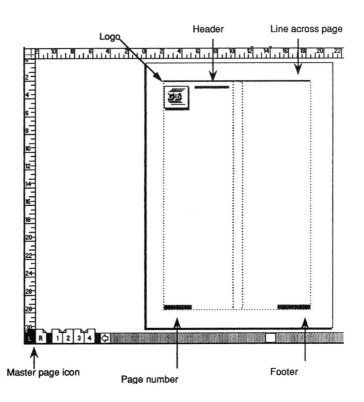

Figure 9.12 Example of a master page

 Your turn

Select a magazine. Find the page where the publishing details are printed.
  a Who is the Editor (or Editor-in-Chief) of the magazine?
  b What other positions (for example, Production Editor, Art Director) are listed?
  c What type of grid has been used – how many columns? Does this vary throughout the magazine?
  d What is the target audience of the publication?
  e What types of articles appear – features, regular columns, letters etc.?

Making a publication easy to read

The design of any publication should make the articles easy to read. There are a number of techniques that can help make it readable.

Headlines

Headlines attract readers to an article. To be effective, they need to stand out and must be much larger in size than the body text, have a `weight` that provides a contrast to the body text and be well written to lead the reader into the article. Weight refers to the thickness of type. Using lower case letters helps to make the headline more readable.

Sub-headings

Sub-headings are used to break up text in an article and to provide cues to the reader about the content of the article. Sub-headings use a larger type size than body text and, like headlines, should stand out. A sub-heading should not be put near the bottom of a column or a page.

Pull quotes

A pull quote is a quotation from the article set in a large font and is used to draw attention to an important part of the article. These are very useful for enticing readers into an article. Figure 9.13(a) shows an example of a pull quote.

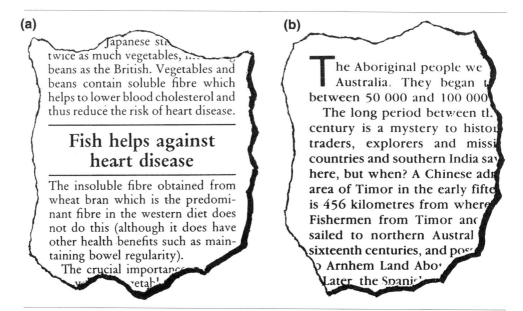

Figure 9.13   **(a)** An example of a pull quote **(b)** A drop cap

Drop caps

A drop cap is a large first letter in an article or paragraph. Its function is to provide a visual cue about the article and to force white space around paragraphs. Drop caps can be quite difficult to create. Figure 9.13(b) shows an example of a paragraph starting with a drop cap.

Graphic images

Visual images to be used in publications should be chosen carefully. Every image should tell a story or add to the text. The graph or photograph that makes the most impact should be chosen. Often a pie chart of figures used for comparison can make more impact than a table showing figures only.

Photographs should be cropped and resized to achieve maximum effect. Choose one large and two small photographs rather than three photographs of the same size.

A caption is text that describes a photograph or illustration. A caption is used to tie together the text and the graphic image. Captions are usually placed either under the image or to its right or left.

People's eyes tend to move from the top left to the bottom right of a page. Visuals can be used to create interest in parts of the page that are often otherwise ignored. See Figure 9.14 for a diagram of this page layout.

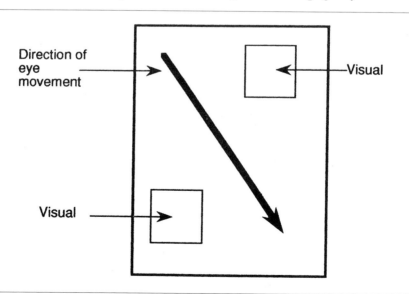

Figure 9.14   Page layout creating interest for the eye.

Your turn

1 Examine a copy of a current newspaper and find two examples of the use of a drop cap and a pull quote.
2 Find three different examples of pull quotes in magazines and newspapers.
3 Examine the front page of a newspaper and answer the following questions.
  a How many photographs are there?
  b Which photograph is the biggest on the page? Where is it located?
  c Do the photographs have captions? If they do, where are they placed in relation to the photographs?

Review questions

1 What is a pull quote? Why is it used?
2 Why use headlines?
3 What is a grid? Write down the name of a publication that uses a three column grid.

Tasks

1 Prepare a leaflet for the sale of a house in a forthcoming auction. The leaflet is to be printed on A4 sized paper. Include some or all of the following details in your leaflet:

  ◆ name and business details of the estate agent selling the property
  ◆ description of the interior layout of the house
  ◆ description of the style of house
  ◆ number of rooms
  ◆ size of the garden
  ◆ the sale is to be by auction, noting the date and time of the auction.

  Your leaflet could include a graphic illustration or photograph of the house. You could also include a sketch of the house that you have created using a graphics program.

2 Prepare a leaflet for a concert by your favourite group or artist. Include some or all of the following details in your leaflet:

  ◆ date, time and location of the concert
  ◆ where tickets can be purchased
  ◆ supporting artists if any
  ◆ nature of the concert
  ◆ price of the tickets
  ◆ names of any sponsoring companies or organisations.

3 Keep a file of documents produced using desk top publishing. Use them to identify the features of both good and bad design.

4 Use a desktop publishing package to create a:
  ◆ class newsletter
  ◆ family newsletter
  ◆ business card
  ◆ curriculum vitae for yourself including a photograph.

10 The information superhighway

What is the information superhighway?

The information superhighway refers to the network services which are available to homes, schools and businesses. It includes cable television, video on demand and interactive home shopping, as well as computer networks.

For most people, the information superhighway refers to the Internet – a network of computer networks.

What is a computer network?

A computer network can span the whole world or a single room. Many schools and businesses use computer networks. A network is made up of:

◆ nodes
◆ connection between the nodes,
  e.g. fibre optic cables, coaxial
  cable, twisted pair wire
◆ computer software to allow
  connections.

A node on a network is any device that is connected to the network.

It can be a:

◆ computer
◆ printer
◆ hard disk.

Why have networks?

Networks allow computer users to share information and centralise file management and maintenance tasks. Networks also allow resources such as:

◆ printers
◆ large storage devices such as hard
  disks
◆ CD ROMs
◆ backup devices
◆ large files
  to be shared by users.

A network can be as simple as two computers connected together to share files. When files are shared, both computers must devote some of their time to managing those files, which can slow down the performance of the computer. A small network might be used to share a laser printer. Figure 10.1 shows a diagram of two computers and a printer in a network.

Figure 10.1   Two computers and a laser printer in a network

Local Area Network

A local area network or LAN is a communications system that is used in a physically limited area, e.g. in a school or an office. An important component of a LAN is a file server. A file server is a program that runs on a computer on the network, thereby allowing multiple users to access disks. It controls the retrieval and storage of files by specified users. It includes security aspects to allow only authorised use of the files. A file server usually needs a dedicated computer to operate if effectively.

The software that runs a file server is very complex and may require a specialist to operate it effectively. Novell and Appleshare are examples of file server software.

A print server is hardware and software that allow users to access printers and to control queues when a number of people are wanting to use a printer at the same time.

The nodes on a network have to be connected in some way. The connection can be by cable – or copper wire – or it can be wireless, using infra-red rays or a radio frequency.

Figure 10.2 is a diagram of a LAN.

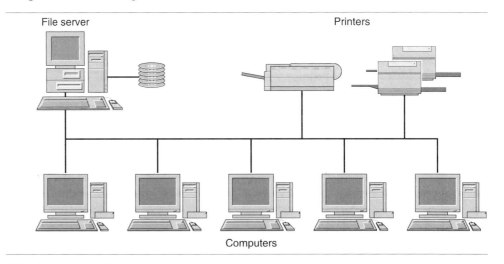

Figure 10.2   A local area network

Your turn

Investigate a local area network to which you have access.

   a What is the name of the software that is used by the file server?

   b How many computers are on the network?

   c What other devices, including printers, are on the network?

What is electronic mail?

Electronic mail allows people to exchange messages or documents within a computer network. An electronic mail system is made up of:

- users of the system
- a computer network
- computer software.

What can it do?

Electronic mail systems allow users to:

- create and send messages
- store messages
- receive and read messages
- reply to messages
- send documents.

Each user on the system has a unique name so that he or she may be identified. Figure 10.3 shows some users of an electronic mail system.

Figure 10.3 Users of an electronic mail system

How does it work?

Electronic mail is similar to using mail boxes at a post office. People create documents and send them to an electronic mail address. The messages are stored in an electronic mail box and the receivers check their mail boxes. They are able to read the messages on-screen and may print them, store them or reply immediately.

Files which are saved can be shared by people, thus allowing a number of people to work on the one project together.

The delivery of messages can be monitored. You can find out the status of messages that have been sent – whether they have been received and read.

Using electronic mail to send a message

To send an electronic mail message, the following must be done:

- log on to the system using your name on the users list
- enter a password, if you have one, to access the system
- choose the user or users to whom the message is to be sent
- create the message and then send it.

Figure 10.4 is an example of a mail window in which a message has been created. The buttons along the top are used to carry out the following functions:

- Address – used to find the address of the person who will receive the mail
- Options – sets the priority on the mail message
- Save As – saves the message on disk
- Print – prints the message on a printer
- Send – send the mail message to the receiver
- Attach – includes another file with the mail message
- Note – which allows a note to be attached to the message
- Detach – removes a file you have attached with the mail message.

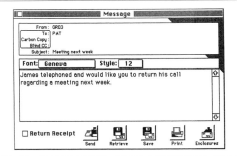

Figure 10.4   A mail window

Using electronic mail to receive a message

When a message is sent, the receiver is notified. If he or she is not logged on to the network at the time, then notification is given at the time of the next log on.

Figure 10.5 shows a file cabinet of mail messages. Each of the folders serves a different purpose:

- Drafts – messages that have been created but not sent are stored here
- Inbox – messages received but not read are stored here
- Mail – stores messages that have been read
- Outbox – stores messages that have been sent.

The buttons along the top are used to carry out the following functions:

- Read New – displays new messages that have been received
- Create – provides the form to create a message
- Reply – provides a form to reply to a message that has been received
- Forward – sends the message to someone else on the mail system
- Send – sends a message
- File In – creates a folder into which a message may be saved
- Print – prints the message on a printer
- Delete – deletes the selected message.

All electronic mail systems carry out similar tasks, but the way they look and how the tasks are carried out may vary.

Figure 10.5   File cabinet

Including sound

Some mail systems allow the inclusion of sound as part of the message. This is called VOICE MAIL. In this case, a message is recorded on the computer and saved as a file. The person to whom the message is sent can play the sound to hear the message.

Your turn

Is an electronic mail system used at your school? If so, what is the name of the software used? Can students send mail messages to:

◆ other students   ◆ teachers?

If you have access to an electronic mail system ask permission to:

◆ send a message to one of the   reply to it
  other students in your class   ◆ delete a message you have
◆ get one of your fellow students to   received after you have read it.
  send you a message, read it and

Using a telephone

A modem is a device that allows a computer to use a telephone line to establish links with another computer.

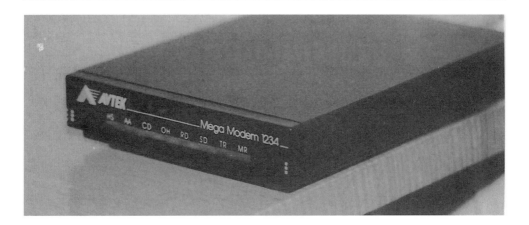

A modem. It needs to be connected to both a telephone and a computer

How is a modem used?

A modem is connected to both a computer and a telephone line. It is used to access other computer networks which are not connected by cable.

The following is required to use a modem:

◆ a computer   ◆ a telephone

◆ a modem   ◆ communications software.

Figure 10.6 shows computers communicating using modems and a telephone line.

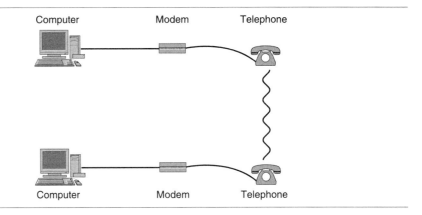

Figure 10.6   Computers communicating using modem and telephone lines

The first time a modem is used, the communications settings must be set up correctly. Figure 10.7 shows the settings using a modem to connect to a remote network. Once the settings are correct, they may be stored as a file and used repeatedly.

The baud rate refers to the speed of transmission of the file over the telephone line. In this case, it is set to 2400 bits per second. This means that 2400 bits per second of data are transmitted on the telephone line. The modem uses the normal telephone network for connection, local calls are charged at the same rate as a standard telephone call. However, care needs to be taken when dialling long distance with STD calls or overseas with IDD calls as the telephone charges can quickly become quite high if long calls are made.

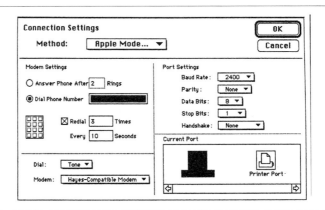

Figure 10.7   Modem settings screen

What is a bulletin board?

A bulletin board is a device which allows users to leave information for others to read. It is the electronic equivalent of a noticeboard.

Notices that may be of interest are available on the bulletin board. Anyone with access to the bulletin board can check the messages and take action if they are interested. Many different bulletin boards are set up to allow people to exchange information on topics of mutual interest.

Users connect to a bulletin board using a modem and communications software.

What is BT Mailbox Service?

BT Mailbox Service is a business communications service which provides electronic mail, access to Fax and X400 messaging. It is compatible with electronic mail systems operating in 24 countries around the world. The service provides a PC-based message management package providing users with a simple message managing system. Using their own word processor a user can create and edit messages and then send them automatically to all clients or employees from their own database automatically. It is easy to receive messages. BT charge for both the software packages and using the system to send and store messages but business users find it a more efficient method of sending error free messages to a large customer or employee database.

What is the Internet?

The Internet is a massive world-wide network of computers. It is a network of networks, in which computers communicate world-wide using phone lines, coaxial cable and a variety of other media. Many of the computers act as file servers allowing users to connect to them and to retrieve and/or store files. Every day, over twenty million users in more than fifty countries connect to the Internet.

There are various features available, including:

E-mail

This lets you send and receive messages to and from other users regardless of where they are or what type of computer they use. Both the sender and receiver of the mail must have an electronic mail or email address. An Internet address is in the form:

BluePeter@bbc.co.uk

Where 'BluePeter' is the name which identifies the person and 'bbc.co.uk' identifies the address.

News groups

Information is distributed and exchanged through news groups. Users can contribute to topics of interest and have questions answered.

File transfer

File Transfer Protocol or FTP allows users to send or retrieve files to other computers. There are many public access services which enable the transfer of files. The files may include text, images, sounds, applications, games and software update. Many of these are protected by copyright, which restricts use of them.

Search Engines

Software called search engines such as 'Yahoo', 'Infoseek' and 'Web Crawler' allow information to be searched for and retrieved even if users do not know where it is stored. This is achieved by entering key words.

Logging on to other computers

A service called Telnet allows users to log on to other computers and use them as if they were on their own local area networks. However, you must have an account with that computer to be able to log on.

Many library catalogues and online databases can be accessed in such a way. Some services charge a fee for access, and some do not.

Using the World Wide Web

The World Wide Web is a body of information presented on the Internet network that is linked via hypertext. Hypertext allows one piece of information to be linked to another piece of information in the system. This allows the user to select the path of his or her choice.

The World Wide Web is a series of pages which are linked by hypertext buttons. Each button takes the user to the next piece of information.

Many organisations provide their own home page for access on the World Wide Web. Figure 10.8 shows the home page for Blue Peter. Each shield is a hypertext button. Clicking on a shield takes the user to a new page. By clicking on 'Coming Up' for example, the user is given information about this week's programmes. Each underlined word 'Big Bash' is another hypertext button.

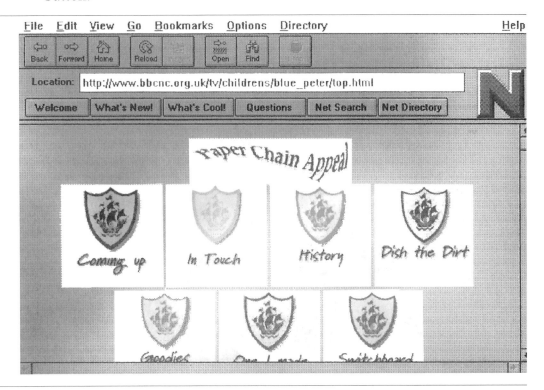

Figure 10.8 Blue Peter home page

Coming Up On Blue Peter

26th-29th October

The **CBBC Big Bash** at the N.E.C. in BirminghaM is on from the
26th to 29th October.

11th October 1995

Blue Peter Launches The Biggest Ever Asthma Survey

As part of Asthma Week, Blue Peter is asking its millions of viewers to take part in the
biggest ever survey of childhood asthma. The survey will provide the best answer yet
to questions like "Do you get bullied because of your asthma?" or "Does your asthma
make you miss PE lessons?".

The media has often reported that asthma is on the increase and during the long, hot
summer much of th blame was put on car exhausts and pollution. But the latest
research indicates that dust mites in the home could be the biggest culprit in
triggering asthma attacks. Blue Peter films with a Southampton family who have
changed their home completely to reduce the possibility of dust mites, and finds out
why one of the children puts his teddy in the freezer every day.

Blue Peter is working with the National Asthma campaign to produce the survey form.

Internet users will be able to complete the form which will be on the In Touch page as
soon as the survey is released.

You can contact the Blue Peter team via e-mail at BluePeter@bbc.co.uk

Figure 10.9 'Coming Up' page

Surfing the net

Hypertext buttons allow you to move around the world searching for
information. Each site has a World Wide Web address which can be used.

How do I get an address?

There are a number of organisations that provide access to the Internet.
Users can subscribe on payment of a fee to those organisations to get access.
Subscription access usually allows a limited number of hours access per week
or per month. After that access is used, a fee is charged at a set rate. There is
usually a peak rate and an off-peak rate. Once you have access, you have your
own Internet address.

Many schools and educational institutions have set up their own Internet
node and provide access to students. This is called a 'point of presence'.

Your turn

1 Does your school use the Internet for communicating with students in other schools? List three projects which could involve collaborative use of the Internet by students from your school and another school.
2 Find out the places where you could gain access to the Internet, e.g. school, home, your parents' workplace, the local library, a cafe.

Review questions

1 Give three reasons why people use the Internet.
2 What are the components of a computer network?
3 What is meant by the terms:
◆ hypertext   ◆ World Wide Web   ◆ 'surfing the net'.

Tasks

1 Use electronic mail to try and make contact with an expert who can help you to find out information for a project at school. Try and set up a list of experts you can consult when you need help. Your parents, relatives and friends may be able to help you make contact with people who can assist you.
2 Many newspapers and television programmes have home pages on the World Wide Web. Try to access the home page of a newspaper. What kinds of stories are accessible? Can you see the compete newspaper for any given day?
3 If you intend studying at a university after you leave school, see if you can access the home page for that university. Use it to help you find out information about the courses you are interested in studying.

Multimedia

11

What is multimedia?

Multimedia combines different media in one computer application. The user can interact by navigating through the content of the application using a mouse, a touch screen or some other pointing device. Many games are examples of multimedia applications. Multimedia applications can be made up of:

- text – as produced by a word processor
- sound – music, recorded voices, noises
- graphics – drawings, paintings, scanned images, photographs, still video images
- animations – created on a computer
- video sequences – digitised and stored on a hard disk or CD ROM.

Why use multimedia?

Multimedia is popular because it provides an effective and stimulating means of communication. Multimedia applications are usually open-ended and non-linear. A videotape is viewed from start to finish, whereas a multimedia production can easily move from on topic to another by clicking on a button. Hypertext allows on piece of information to be linked to another piece of information in the system, thus enabling the user to select the path of his or her choice.

Multimedia may be used to present information in formats which are entertaining and enriching – for example, access to archival film clips can bring to life historical events for the multimedia user.

Using multimedia applications

A multimedia application is usually made up of a carefully designed screen which contains:

◆ buttons
◆ searching mechanisms
◆ hot spots that link information.

By clicking on the buttons, the user moves through the application. Each button has a script which it executes. Some standard buttons appear at the top of each screen – for example, in Figure 11.1, there are six standard buttons. Other buttons are used to show photographs, maps, videos and animations, and to play sounds and recordings. For the 'Scotland' entry, there are several such buttons – for maps, photographs, music etc.

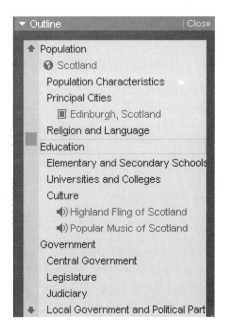

Figure 11.1   Scotland entry in Microsoft Encarta

Hot spots are often words that are printed in bold or italics. Clicking on these highlighted words takes the user to related specific information. In Figure 11.2, the hot spots (equator, solstice and Tropics) in the entry 'Tropic of Capricorn' are underlined. After choosing a hot spot, readers are usually able to return to the previous screen.

Tropic of Capricorn, parallel of latitude at 23° 27' south of the *equator*, delineating the southernmost point at which the sun can appear directly overhead at noon. At the tropic of Capricorn, the sun's rays strike the earth vertically on one day a year—the winter *solstice* (on or about December 22). The tropic of Capricorn marks the southern boundary of the *Tropics* or Torrid Zone.

A hot spot in
Microsoft Encarta

Figure 11.2

What is a multimedia computer?

A multimedia computer consists of:

- a monitor
- a CPU (central processing unit)
- large amounts of RAM (random access memory)
- a CD ROM drive
- a high-quality monitor
- a sound card
- speakers.

The sound card allows digitised sound to be amplified and played through the speakers. For quick and effective display, colour images and video sequences require a large amount of RAM. The computer processor also needs to be fast to ensure that the video images are not distorted or jerky. Multimedia is typically delivered on CD ROM. In the future though, it will be delivered across fast computer networks, which will also deliver video images on demand.

What is CD ROM?

'CD ROM' stands for 'compact disk read-only memory'. A CD ROM looks just like a music compact disk. Large amounts of data may be recorded on CD ROMs, which are read using low-powered laser beams. Being a read-only device, data on a CD ROM cannot be erased.

When attached to a computer, a CD ROM is like a large hard disk which can be removed easily. A special disk drive is needed to access it, which looks like a music compact disk player. However, a CD player cannot play a CD ROM, although a CD ROM drive can play music CDs, providing speakers are attached to the computer.

A special disk drive for CD ROMs is needed if a computer does not have one built in

Your turn

1 Visit your school library or local library and see what CD ROMs are available for use.
  a List the names of ten different CD ROMs that you can find.
  b Classify them using the following categories:

  ◆ encyclopaedia
  ◆ dictionary
  ◆ newspapers
  ◆ magazines
  ◆ games
  ◆ collections of images
  ◆ collections of sounds.

  c Which of these would be classified as multimedia titles?
  d Review one of the times and comment on its function and usefulness.

2 Find an example of a computer that uses multimedia:

  ◆ in an information kiosk
  ◆ in a game
  ◆ as a part of an encyclopaedia.

What are multimedia computers used for?

Because all kinds of information can be stored on CD ROMs, multimedia computers are used in a variety of places by many people. Some common uses are:

◆ business training
◆ entertainment
◆ music
◆ films
◆ reference titles
◆ talking books.

A multimedia encyclopaedia

'Microsoft Encarta' is a multimedia encyclopaedia which provides a large amount of information. It includes:

◆ text – 27,000 entries
◆ audio – recorded sounds, including speeches
◆ scanned photographs
◆ maps
◆ animations
◆ video clips
◆ charts
◆ links between selected terms.

  Figure 11.3 shows the entry for Jane Austen. Note the following features:

◆ navigation buttons across the top of the screen
◆ buttons with pull down menus to allow printing etc.
◆ buttons to indicate a photograph.

Figure 11.3

Learn a language

Learning a language can be difficult, memorising vocabulary, struggling to pronounce words without a teacher at hand all the time.

Interactive language learning provides challenges at all levels, working through exercises which use the facilities of audio for perfecting pronunciation. You can record your own voice and then compare it to a native speaker, breaking down the speech to single words or even individual syllables to aid learning.

Interactive language packages typically include:

- ◆ Games to perfect vocabulary
- ◆ Describing people and places
- ◆ Describing activities
- ◆ Charts to show progress

- ◆ Narrating a story
- ◆ Number work
- ◆ Tests against the clock

One such package is 'The Syracuse Language Systems' where you select a topic and then an appropriate level at which to work. An example of the menu is shown in Figure 11.4.

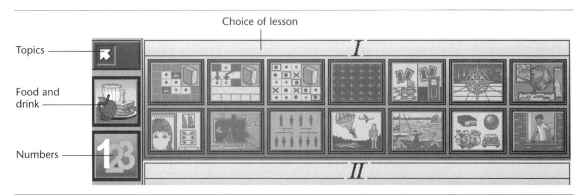

Figure 11.4 Example of an Interactive Language package

Europe in the Round

The CD ROM 'Europe in the Round' is a multimedia profile of the European Union. It provides economic data about all member countries including employment and output statistics. It is possible to view data on individual countries or compare one country with another.

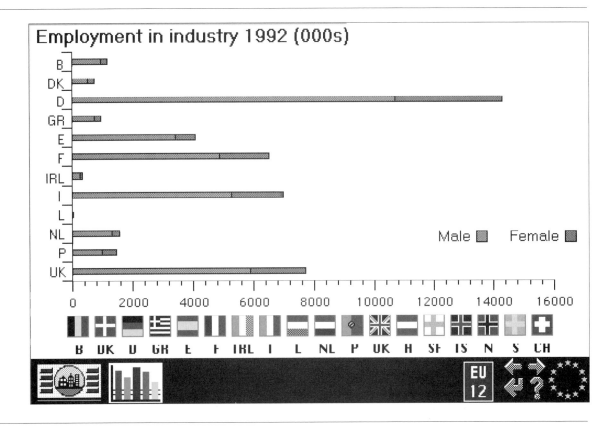

Figure 11.5   Statistics from 'Europe in the Round'

Your turn

1 'Microsoft Encarta'
   a Look at the video of the Berlin Wall. When was the Berlin Wall constructed? What did President Kennedy take pride in saying? The Wall was demolished immediately before the immigration barriers between East and West Berlin were dropped. When did these events occur?
   b According to 'Encarta', what is the population of Sydney?
   c What is the length of the coastline of Australia? What is the highest mountain peak in Australia and how high is it?
2 Find out what sorts of interactive language learning packages your school uses.
   a Can you record your own voice?
   b Can you compare it to a native speaker?
   c What advantages do your think there are in using computers to aid language learning?
   d What disadvantages do you think there are in using computer language learning?

3 If your library has a copy of 'Europe in the round' answer the following questions:
Use 'background information' and 'EU information' (click on EU button) find out?

   a The total civilian population in employment and the percentage female employment for the EU?

   b The percentage of the EU's usable arable land under permanent grassland and how many litres of wine are produced by the EU per year?

   c By how many million the number of Spanish speakers exceeds French speakers in the EU?

   d Which EU country has the most kilometres of motorway?

   e What is the birth rate, per 1000, in Ireland and Greece?

Creating multimedia

To create a multimedia application you need:

◆ an authoring tool
◆ a range of different types of data.

Such a creation, which is made up of a number of screens, sometimes called cards, is called a presentation. The cards or screens in a presentation are called a stack or a book.

Authoring tools

An authoring tool is a software package that allows a user to create a multimedia presentation. It generally provides:

◆ the ability to link together related information
◆ the ability to integrate a range of media created elsewhere
◆ drawing and paint tools
◆ the ability to create backgrounds.

Types of data

Data can be presented in various forms:

◆ text
◆ images
◆ sounds
◆ animations
◆ video.

Text

This is usually created in a word processor where the spelling can be checked. It may be imported or copied into the multimedia application.

Graphics

Images are prepared using graphics programs which can then be used in multimedia applications (see Chapter 6).

Photographs can be added to multimedia applications by using:

◆ a scanner – which allows digitised images to be imported into the multimedia application, where they can be enhanced and resized

◆ a photo CD – which contains photographs that can be loaded directly into the multimedia application. Images can then be enhanced, resized and cropped

◆ a digital camera (ION) which records images straight into a computer's memory. The photographs can then be loaded into the multimedia application and enhanced, resized and cropped.

Sounds

Sounds may be created by the user. A control panel is used to play and record a sound, which can then be cut, copied and pasted in the same way as for text.

Some applications include a range of sounds which may be added to a presentation. For example, the Oxford University Press 'Télé-Textes' CD ROM offers a voice-recording facility which allows students to record and play back their own commentary over the video sequences.

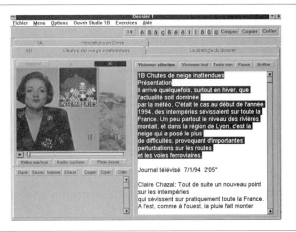

Figure 11.6

Animations

Animations may be created to imported. Kid Pix Deluxe allows the user to produce an animation by choosing a stamp and then dragging a path for the image to follow. Authoring packages such as HyperCard and Toolkit enable the creation of images.

Videos

Video may be used in a multimedia presentation. In order to do this, a video needs to be digitised and compressed to store it on a hard disk. Digitised video may come from:

◆ clip videos on a CD ROM

◆ the process of capturing video.

To capture video images you need:

◆ a high-powered computer
◆ a large hard disk
◆ a special digitiser card in the computer

◆ a video player connected to the computer
◆ software to capture the video
◆ software to edit the video.

Figure 11.7 shows how text and video run alongside each other on the 'Télé-Textes' CD ROM.

Figure 11.7

Designing your own multimedia presentation

A presentation is made up of a number of screens, sometimes called cards. It typically includes graphics and text elements with buttons for navigation. The placement on screen of the different media used in a multimedia application requires thought and planning. For example, the text font must be easily readable and the colours appealing to the eye. The design and screen location of these elements is also important as it affects the linkages between screens and the ease of use of the presentation.

Linking the screens

The designer must consider how a user will interact with the presentation and link the screens accordingly. A multimedia presentation can be designed so that it is flexible to use yet structured. Figure 11.8 gives an example of how a main menu card links to an opening screen and three topic areas.

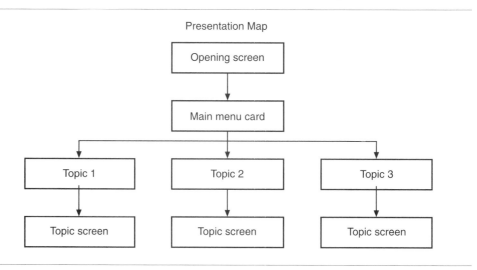

Figure 11.8

Background and screen layers

A presentation often includes a background layer upon which the topic screens are superimposed. Figure 11.10 is from the 'HyperCard Tour Stack', which shows a background layer and a screen or card layer.

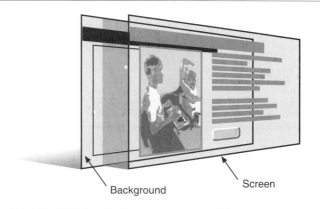

Figure 11.9

Navigation buttons

A button is a screen area which, activate, performs a pre-defined action. Buttons are the most common method of linking screens together. They are used to move forwards and backwards through screens.

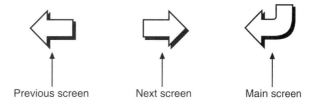

Figure 11.10

Buttons can be different sizes and have different pictures or icons attached to them. Some of the icons which are attached to HyperCard stack are shown in Figure 11.11.

Figure 11.11

Your turn

1 Using Figure 11.13 as an example, design a card which shows a fellow student's image and provides text about that student.
   a Include a background layer which shows the name of your school and class level.
   b Draw buttons for navigating from one card/screen to the next.

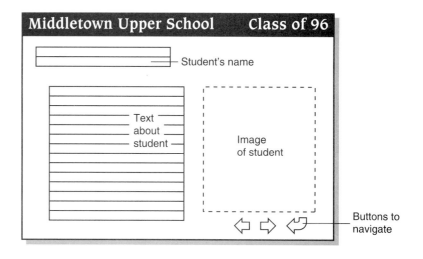

Figure 11.12 An example of a background card

   c Using Figure 11.12 as an example, draw a picture and write the text for your card screen. Note how, in the example, the background and screen layer are combined.

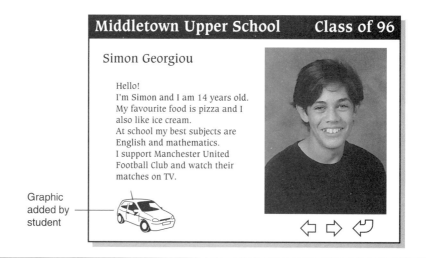

Figure 11.13 An example of combined background and screen layers

2 Create a multimedia family album. You could include information about each member of your family, photographs, a short recorded speech by each

member and, perhaps, segments of a family video. You could use Hypercard or Toolbox to provide a card for each family member and link the cards together with buttons.

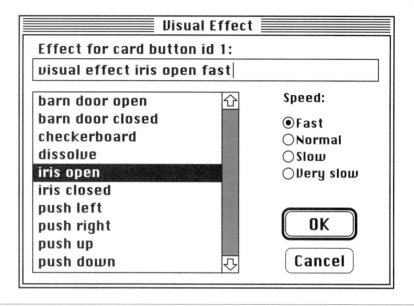

Figure 11.14   Card transition effect

Review questions

1   What is digitised sound?
2   How much data can a CD ROM store? How much sound can be recorded on a CD?
3   Give your reasons why CD ROMs are used with computers.
4   What is an authoring tool? Name two examples of authoring tools.
5   What is hypertext? Why is it important in multimedia applications?
6   What is a button? What are buttons used for in multimedia productions?

Task

Create a multimedia Christmas message to send to your relatives. Include a digitised image of yourself plus a recorded message.

Putting it all together

Integrated software

Integrated software is a single working environment made up of a number of tools. These tools are often called modules. Most integrated packages include:

- word processor
- spreadsheet
- database
- communications module
- drawing package
- presentation package.

The packages are selected using icons, called the 'graphic user interface' (GUI). Figure 12.1 shows the GUI for popular Microsoft packages.

Figure 12.1   Part of 'Microsoft Office' (GUI)

Information can be shared between single applications using a variety of methods An integrated package can share the information using 'cut and paste' and 'copy and paste'.

Why use an integrated package?

An integrated package is used because of:

- its usefulness – the features of separate applications are combined into one application
- the ease of sharing information between modules
- its price – an integrated package usually costs less than a number of different applications
- the common commands, menus and function keys that apply across modules.

What are the disadvantages of integrated packages?

The disadvantages of integrated packages include:

- features – the modules do not have all the features of dedicated software packages
- user needs – not all the modules may be required
- overall quality – one module may be very weak and thus limit the overall effectiveness of the package.

Your turn

1 What integrated package(s) can you use at school or home?
2 What modules are in the package?
3 What advantages does an integrated package have over separate applications?
4 Find an example of an advertisement for the sale of a computer with an integrated pack, usually called a 'bundled deal'.

Why share data?

The tools of one module can make information created by another more meaningful. A word processor is suited to text and formatting, a spreadsheet for calculations, tables and charts and a database for sorting and arranging of data.

How is information shared?

An integrated package makes it easy to use information created in another module by:

- using cut and paste or copy and paste
- setting up a document to access information from another module.

Word processors can usually merge information. The integrated package has the advantage of using an existing database within the same package.

Information created in one module can be transferred to another module, modified and, if necessary, transferred back. Within Microsoft Office you can work on other applications through 'active windows' without leaving the main application you are using. A word processing document is often the result of bringing together material from other modules.

Creating a letter using the word processor and database

Using a word processor and a database to create a letter is called 'mail merge'. 'Mail merge' means that the same letter apart from personal details can be sent to a number of people. The steps to mail merge are:

- prepare the body of the letter using the word processor
- link the word processor and the database using appropriate commands
- create a database report for
- personal details, such as names and addresses
- decide where in the letter the data is to be included
- print the letters using the word processor.

A letter produced this way is sometimes call a 'form' letter. Figure 12.2 shows how the database records are incorporated with the form letter.

A person writing to a number of people about the same topic could use the same letter with the name and address details read from a database. Many large organisations create personalised letters in this way.

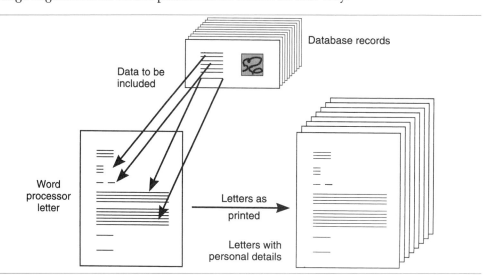

Figure 12.2 Creation of a form letter

Example – Creating a form letter for a family reunion

You have been asked to help organise a family reunion. One of the tasks is to contact family members and tell them about the reunion. Figure 12.3 shows a sample database used to record the names and addresses of the family members. Some of this information will be merged with a letter telling them about the reunion.

A letter is created with places allocated for the data to be merged. Included in the letter are the places for the database information.

In some software, the fields to be merged are shown on screen enclosed within special characters. The merge characters for Microsoft Word are <<and>>. For example, the address details could appear in the word processing document as:

<<title>> <<given>> <<family>>

<<no>> <<street>>

<<town>> <<country>> <<postcode>>

Figure 12.4 shows the letter printed using the word processor. To print the letter and include the database information requires a 'Print Merge' command rather than the normal 'Print' command.

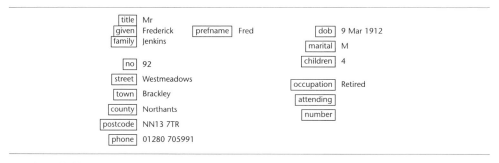

Figure 12.3 Database fields and information

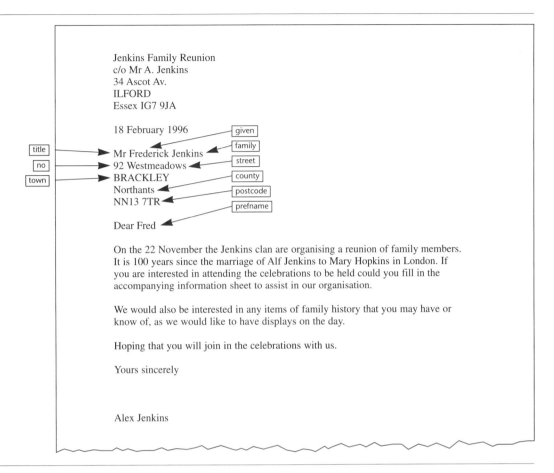

Figure 12.4   Mail merge letter ready to post

 Your turn

1 From the merged letter in Figure 12.4 identify the database fields that have been included in the letter.

2 List possible uses for 'mail merge' letters. Consider how a school, charity, sporting organisation or individuai could use mail merge.

3 Find examples of mail merged letters that have come to your household. How can you tell if a letter has been mail merged?

4 You are going to send a personalised letter with news about your family to your friends with your Christmas cards this year. List the fields that should be contained in the database file. What information would you include in the letter? How would you set up the database and word processor to merge the information?

Adding a graphic to a document

A graphic can be included in a word processing document.
The main steps are:

- create a graphic in a graphics program
- copy the graphic and paste it into the word processor
- save the graphic file in a form that can be read by the word processor.

The graphic can then be incorporated into a letter. Figure 12.5 shows a graphic included in the letter for the family reunion.

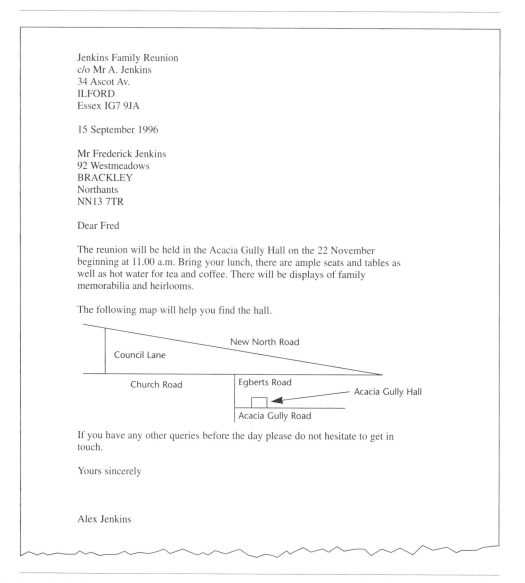

Jenkins Family Reunion
c/o Mr A. Jenkins
34 Ascot Av.
ILFORD
Essex IG7 9JA

15 September 1996

Mr Frederick Jenkins
92 Westmeadows
BRACKLEY
Northants
NN13 7TR

Dear Fred

The reunion will be held in the Acacia Gully Hall on the 22 November beginning at 11.00 a.m. Bring your lunch, there are ample seats and tables as well as hot water for tea and coffee. There will be displays of family memorabilia and heirlooms.

The following map will help you find the hall.

If you have any other queries before the day please do not hesitate to get in touch.

Yours sincerely

Alex Jenkins

Figure 12.5 Letter including graphic

Your turn

Prepare an invitation to your next birthday party using a word processor and graphics you have created. Personalise the invitations for each participant by using database information.

a Create suitable graphics in a graphics program. Clip art could be also used. Include a map showing guests how to get to the party.

b Create the text in the word processor. Include the date, address, drop off and pick up times, any special details of the party (for example, if it is a fancy dress party or sleep over).

c Create a database with appropriate fields such as name and address.

d Print the letter with the merged details.

The word processor and the spreadsheet

A budget requiring calculations and analysis could be prepared in a spreadsheet. The completed budget and graphs created in the spreadsheet could be copied to a word processor. The word processor can then be used to explain the features of the budget. The word processor can then be used for the class history excursion to the Black Country Museum as it appears in the spreadsheet.

Budget: Class history excursion	
Expenses	
	£
Coach	185
Photocopy of materials	30
Entry to Black Country Museum	118.5
Insurance	4.80
Food and drink	105
Total	£416.30
Number of students	30
Cost per student	**£13.88**

These cells contain formulae

Figure 12.6 History visit budget

When the material is copied from the spreadsheet to the word processor it will be copied as it appears on screen, that is, only the values will be transferred. Figure 12.7 shows how the budget could appear in a word processed document. The document has been prepared for the school bursar to show the cost items and how the cost per student has been calculated.

Budget: Class history excursion	
Expenses	
	$
Coach	185
Photocopy of materials	30
Entry to Black Country Museum	118.5
Insurance	4.80
Food and drink	105
Total	£416.30
Number of students	30
Cost per student	**£13.88**

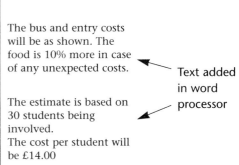

The bus and entry costs will be as shown. The food is 10% more in case of any unexpected costs.

The estimate is based on 30 students being involved.
The cost per student will be £14.00

Text added in word processor

Figure 12.7 Budget with comments

Your turn

1 Enter the budget into the spreadsheet module of an integrated package. Make sure that the cell containing the 'Total' £416.30 and the cell containing the 'Cost per student' contain formula to give the amounts shown in Figure 12.7.
2 Listed below are some other possible ways of conducting the excursion. Adjust the spreadsheet to take account of the new arrangements. Copy the spreadsheet to the word processor and add a comment to explain the budget and the arrangements in a document to be given to the bursar.
   a Students bring a packed lunch so no food is provided by the school.
   b Students visit 'Cadbury's World' on the same day with an additional cost of £100.50 for entry and £35.00 extra for the hire of the coach.
3 Collect the maximum and minimum temperatures for your city or town over a week. Put the information in the spreadsheet, draw a line chart, transfer the information to the word processor and comment upon the results.
4 Select ten grocery items and compare the prices at two supermarkets. Put the information into the spreadsheet and calculate the total cost of the items. Transfer the information to the word processor and report on your findings.

The database and the spreadsheet

A database selection or report can be transferred to the spreadsheet. More complex calculations can be performed and the information presented in chart form. Figure 12.8 shows membership details for the Summervale Tennis Club. The details were prepared from a database report. The information could be charted to make it easier to understand. Figure 12.8 also shows how the information can be separated into three charts.

Male chart · Female chart

	Male	Female
Junior	30	17
Under 18	22	24
Open	43	32
Senior	3	9
TOTAL MEMBERS	108	82

Financial
members
chart

Figure 12.8 Financial members of the Summervale Tennis Club, June 1996 and information to be
included in chart form

Figure 12.9 shows how the information about the number of female
members can be charted. The data is selected, the spreadsheet plots the chart
and calculates the percentages. The title has been added by the user.

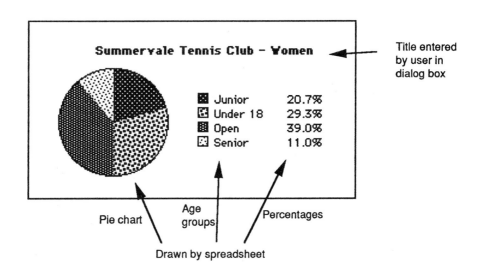

Title entered
by user in
dialog box

Pie chart

Age
groups

Percentages

Drawn by spreadsheet

Figure 12.9 Pie chart of female members

Your turn

1 Which group of female members of the Summervale Tennis Club is the
largest?
2 Why has a pie chart been selected to represent breakdown of female
members?
3 Use a spreadsheet to prepare a pie chart for the men using the figures in
Figure 12.8.
4 Why does a chart enable information to be more easily understood?
   The chart can then be copied and placed in a word processing document
where comments can be added. Figure 12.10 shows the chart with a comment
about the numbers of female members.

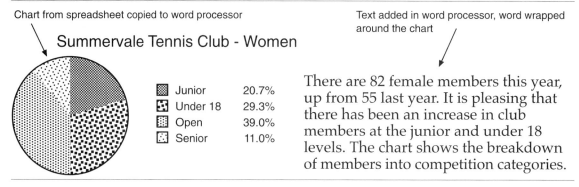

Chart from spreadsheet copied to word processor

Text added in word processor, word wrapped around the chart

Summervale Tennis Club - Women

▨	Junior	20.7%
▨	Under 18	29.3%
▨	Open	39.0%
▨	Senior	11.0%

There are 82 female members this year, up from 55 last year. It is pleasing that there has been an increase in club members at the junior and under 18 levels. The chart shows the breakdown of members into competition categories.

Figure 12.10   Chart with comments added

Selecting an application

A project often includes a number of tasks to be performed requiring more than one software type. For example the organisation of a family reunion could require 'mail merge' as shown above. The following are examples of tasks that need to be done and suggestions regarding the applications to be used.

Tasks to be done	Software (separate application or module of integrated package)
Compile a database of people and relevant personal details. Add to the database as more information becomes available.	Database (Figure 12.2 shows some of the information that could be included)
Send preliminary information and details in a letter and information sheet to those who have a family connection.	Word processor and database (Figure 12.4 shows an example of a letter that could be sent using mail merge)
Prepare an information sheet with the details of the social functions to be held.	Word processor, database report and desktop publishing
Prepare name tags for people attending the reunion.	Database report
Prepare a newsletter for distribution on the day of the reunion.	Word processor, graphics, desktop publishing
Prepare a budget so that costs can be covered by a contribution from participants.	Database, spreadsheet, word processor
Circulate the minutes of the preliminary meetings held to organise the reunion.	Word processor
Create a family tree.	Graphics

Your turn

Which modules of an integrated package could you use for the following tasks?

- write a letter to a friend
- write a letter to a number of friends
- perform calculations on a list of figures
- catalogue your CD collection
- create address labels for envelopes
- keep a running balance of your bank account.

Review questions

1 How can information be shared among the modules of an integrated package?
2 Describe the process of 'mail merge'.

Tasks

1 You have been asked to organise a three-day geography field trip at the end of term. Twenty-five students will attend the field trips. The following tasks need to be carried out:

- collect the names and personal details of students
- prepare and maintain a database for pre-camp organisation and use during the field trip
- prepare a letter with personal
- details for each of the participants and their parents
- prepare a budget listing the costs of the field trip and show how these costs will be covered.

2 Alberts Estate Agents is a well known and long established property company. The company is undergoing a process of modernisation. You have been asked to undertake the following tasks.

- The corporate logo and business stationery are to be changed to reflect the new modern image. The current logo is as follows:

ALBERTS ESTATE AGENTS LTD

The firm's address is 18 Bream Street, Bicester, Oxon OX12 9PK. The phone number is 01869 241153, the mobile phone number is 08500 71108 and the fax number is 01869 232461. The new logo will be used for the letterheads, business cards and other stationery such as promotional leaflets and advertising.

◆ Establish a property price database for their area. Design a database and enter ten pieces of data to test the database. Often this information is reported in the newspaper. Following is an example of a report and possible fields for the database. It might be useful to add other fields such as postcode.

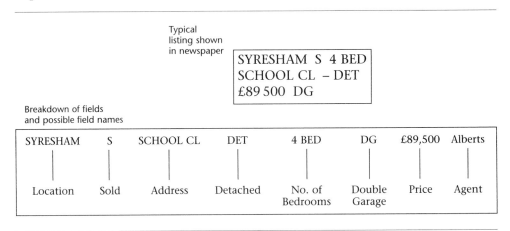

Typical listing shown in newspaper

SYRESHAM S 4 BED
SCHOOL CL – DET
£89 500 DG

Breakdown of fields and possible field names

SYRESHAM	S	SCHOOL CL	DET	4 BED	DG	£89,500	Alberts
Location	Sold	Address	Detached	No. of Bedrooms	Double Garage	Price	Agent

◆ Provide an example of a house plan sketch drawn using a graphics package. The graphic is to be used with a desktop publishing program for advertising brochures for the property.

In small teams:

◆ Prepare a report on the classes use of their leisure time. Each member of the team can investigate a different topic – club, sport, television, hobbies, etc.

Your report could include:

◆ a title page with your names, the report title and a suitable clip art graphic
◆ text prepared with a word processor
◆ graphs showing how students use their free time

◆ what their favourite TV programmes are
◆ scanned in photograph of you enjoying your leisure time

Index